Heavenly Encounters

VOLUME 2

Gerry Dodson with Steve and Tama Lester

ISBN: 1542401615
ISBN 13: 9781542401616

Contents

Acknowledgements

Steve Lester

We would like to extend our sincere thanks to each person who took the time to share his or her testimony for this book. Like the leper who returned to thank Jesus, may you receive the fullness of God's blessing.

Two people were indispensible in this project. Judy Burton and Susan Dodson spent hours typing, proof reading and editing the book. Thanks to both of you!

Most of all, it is the purpose of this book to bring honor to our Lord and Savior Jesus Christ. It is He who makes possible every miracle; particularly the most important miracle of all—eternal life.

Sin (disobedience to God) separates every person from God.

"For all have sinned and come short of the glory of God."

Romans 3:23

"There is none righteous, no not one."

Romans 3:10

"For the wages of sin is death, but the gift of God is eternal life through Jesus Christ our Lord."

Romans 6:23

A person cannot earn salvation by doing good works.

> *"For by grace are ye saved through faith; and that not of yourselves: it is the gift of God: Not of works, lest any man should boast. For we are his workmanship, created in Christ Jesus unto good works, which God hath before ordained that we should walk in them."*

Ephesians 2:8-10

God the Father has provided salvation through His Son, Jesus Christ.

> *"But God demonstrates His own love toward us, in that while we were still sinners, Christ died for us."*

Romans 5:8

> *"The Lord is not slack concerning his promise, as some men count slackness; but is longsuffering to us-ward, not willing that any should perish, but that all should come to repentance."*

II Peter 3:9

> *"For God so loved the world, that he gave his only begotten Son, that whosoever believeth in him should not perish, but have everlasting life. For God sent not his Son into the world to condemn the world; but that the world through him might be saved."* John 3:16,17
> *"We pray you in Christ's stead, be ye reconciled to God. For he hath made him to be sin for us, who knew no sin; that we might be made the righteousness of God in him."*

II Corinthians 5:20,21

What must a person do to be saved?

"He that believeth and is baptized shall be saved; but he that believeth not shall be damned."

Mark 16:16

"That if thou shalt confess with thy mouth the Lord Jesus, and shalt believe in thine heart that God hath raised him from the dead, thou shalt be saved. For with the heart man believeth unto righteousness, and with the mouth confession is made unto salvation."

Romans 10:9 -10

"And it shall come to pass that whosoever calls on the name of the Lord shall be saved."

Acts 2:21

"Thanks be unto God for his unspeakable gift."

II Corinthians 9:15

Forward

Gerry Dodson

*A*fter the release of the book, <u>*Heavenly Encounters*</u>, we had a lot of positive feedback, both oral and written. My daughter-in-law, Susan, and Steve Lester suggested we should publish another book if we could get enough people to share their testimonies. I know that people are inspired and encouraged when they read of God's care for His creation; whether in the small details of life, or in life-threatening situations. I wasn't sure if we could get enough people to share their stories.

One evening I was trying to decide what to do. I really wasn't praying, just weighing the pros and cons. I couldn't come to a clear decision. The next day when I went to the mailbox there was a package that contained a book that I <u>had not</u> ordered. It was a book of testimonies; wonderful stories of God's intervention in the circumstances of people's lives. I can't say for sure that this was a sign from God that we should publish another book, but the timing was very unusual.

I thought of God's instructions for us to share our experiences with the generations that follow us. "*Only take heed to thyself, and keep thy soul diligently, lest thou forget the things which thine eyes have seen, and lest they depart from thy heart all the days of thy life; but teach them to thy sons, and thy son's sons*". Deuteronomy 4:9 KJV

How will the next generation know of God's willingness and power to help us if we fail to tell them?

After receiving the book and reading again the instructions God gives all of us to tell our stories, we decided to publish another book.

My prayer is that you will be blessed and grow in faith by reading the true stories included in this book. We want people to know God still performs miracles. We believe we serve an unchanging Lord and should not question His ability to meet the needs of His people today, as He did in Bible times.

The Lord is Near to the Brokenhearted

Toni McGarry Allen

The LORD is near to the brokenhearted and saves those who are crushed in spirit.

Psalms 34:18

I was awakened from sound sleep by a shrill, loud fire alarm. Nothing seemed out of the ordinary. Down the hallway and into the living room... nothing. Out the back door onto the deck... everything seemed OK. From the back yard I looked up to the roof. Black smoke was pouring from the chimney and ventilation turbines. It becomes real. The house is on fire!

Walking back into the house I called for Molly, the cat, but got no response. A voice in my head said, "Leave the doors open for Molly. Get your purse and car keys. Go to the garage and open the garage door. Back your car out of the garage and away from the house." As if I were floating I did all these things. I moved the car away from the house up under a tree in the front yard.

Dark, black smoke billowed from the turbines and from the vent on the west end of the house. Thick smoke and red flames engulfed the west bedrooms including the room I had been sleeping in just minutes before.

I dialed 911 and gave them all my information. Then I tried to call my daughter, Amy, but could not get the phone to work. Shaking uncontrollably, I began trying to call Tama, my other daughter. A voice said, "Toni, can I help you?" It was Jeff Wright, a local man. How did he get here, I wondered. "Please call Tama and Amy," I said, "for I am shaking too badly to dial the phone." Jeff called the school to let Amy know and our neighbor, Kelly called the forestry department to let Tama know.

Soon, the fire fighters were on the scene doing their job—fighting the fire. I was told later that the garage door almost fell on one of the firemen. Now I wonder how I ever got that garage door open so I could get out of the garage.

My daughters arrived and took control of everything. Tom, my husband, was working in Smithville that morning—about an hour's drive away. Word eventually got to him and I became concerned that he might drive too fast getting home. The girls stayed in contact with him, assuring him that I was OK.

By now the house is a total loss. The yard is full of many people willing to help in any way they can. I was sitting in my car watching the whole scene when a fireman walked over and asked, "Mrs. Allen, are you alright?" "My chest is feeling tight with a lot of pressure," I said. He told me, "I have an ambulance on the way."

My daughters, Amy and Tama, requested the helicopter to be at the airport to airlift me to Texarkana. Dr. Hurley was notified of my condition and soon arrival. I was in the ambulance being prepped to move to the airport when Pastor Terry Bradley's face appeared through the back window with a smile and a thumbs up. I knew he was praying for me.

At the airport I was moved into the helicopter. Small space! One pilot, one assistant, and me. Soon after lifting off the pilot announced that Texarkana was too foggy. We would have to go to Paris instead. "But that is not where my doctor is!" Sorry, but that is where we are taking you.

I was admitted to a room in Paris, TX. In a short while, Tama and Amy arrived at the hospital. They had talked to Dr. Hurley in Texarkana (my regular doctor) and informed him of my condition. Arrangements had been made to move me by ambulance the next morning.

By that afternoon Tom, Steve Smalling (Cowboy) and Steve Lester, my sons-in-law, arrived in Paris to see me. I was glad to see them. Tom was still in dirty work clothes because all of his were destroyed in the fire. Once Tom was assured that I was okay, the two Steves took him to buy some new clothes and a new suitcase, as we didn't know what the next few days had in store for us. Pastor Terry and Sister Kim came by to check on us and pray with us. I am thankful for that.

The next day around 1:00 pm the hospital finally got an ambulance to take me to Texarkana to St. Michael's Hospital. I don't know how long this trip was – I do know the driver seemed to be in a very big hurry: Have you ever ridden in an ambulance on a 12" board, strapped down with the driver weaving in and out of traffic?? This was a "hold on to the board and hope you don't fall off" ride. I am thankful for the paramedic that was stationed behind my head for the ride; she kept an eye on my vital signs. I just closed my eyes and prayed the whole trip. I was never so glad to arrive in Texarkana. *"Do not be anxious about anything, but in everything by prayer and supplication with thanksgiving let your requests be made known to God. And the peace of God, which surpasses all understanding, will guard your hearts and your minds in Christ Jesus."* Philippians 4:6, 7

They wheeled me into the hospital and Dr. Hurley was standing there waiting on me. He said, "Where have you been? I have been waiting 1 ½ days for you!" Immediately they took me to a room and the nurse said, "Are we waiting until tomorrow morning to do this procedure?" Dr. Hurley replied, "No, right now!" After the procedure was completed, Dr. Hurley told the girls his diagnosis was takotsubo cardiomyopathy, also known as *broken heart syndrome*. The upper right part of my heart had "frozen" or wasn't pumping correctly. He shared that women are more likely than men to experience this and most of the time it is brought about by an *emotionally stressful event*. Dr. Hurley told us it would take a few weeks for the heart to return to normal function. I was able to come home in a few days – although home was now a hotel room. *"He heals the broken hearted and binds up their wounds."* Psalms 147:3

I had many heroes on this March day – Jeff Wright, first responders, my neighbor Kelly who called Tama, lots of fire fighters, family, friends, Pilots, nurses, Dr.'s, Pastor Bradley and Sister Kim, Pastor Brian and Pastor Jason, my church family, and Dewayne Clay. I am blessed beyond measure. But the greatest hero of the day was my heavenly Father, my one Savior. He was there every step of the way, never leaving me or forsaking me. His promises are true and He is faithful to His children.

I believe in God the Father.
I believe in Jesus Christ.
I believe in the Holy Spirit.
I believe in the Crucifixion.
I believe that He conquered death.
I believe in the Resurrection.
And He's coming back again.
I BELIEVE.

God's Miraculous Work

Anonymous

*S*eptember 23rd, 2015, I received the phone call. I had been at a national Country Women of the World conference in Tulsa, Oklahoma and was driving home to Broken Bow. About half way home my cell phone rang and my son, David, was calling. When I answered the phone, he had very unexpected news. Genevieve, our daughter-in-law was in ICU at Herman Hospital in Houston, Texas with multiple pulmonary embolisms.

She was also 26 weeks pregnant with our first grandchild and their first baby, a baby boy whose name would be Connor Adam. Our children had waited 13 years for this baby, and just being pregnant seemed like a miracle in itself. But God had more miracles in store.

Of course, when David told me what happened, I was terrified and totally beside myself. I knew when David said "pulmonary embolisms" that Genevieve had blood clots that had gone to her lungs and that her very survival and that of baby Connor was in extreme jeopardy. All the rest of the way home, I cried uncontrollably while I prayed fervently. I honestly don't know how I managed to drive home through the tears. It was beyond imagining or any understanding why God would finally grant us this joy of baby Connor only to have something so life threatening occur.

While still on the road, I called everyone I could think of asking for prayer. My sister in Florida put the word out to her prayer chain. My church family began to pray. After calling my nephew, he made immediate contacts with his church family for prayers. And local friends stopped in the middle of their class at the Quilt Shoppe and had prayer for Genevieve and Connor. Prayers

5

were winging their way to heaven from family, friends, and prayer warriors I had never met and may never meet. Prayers by so many people were already in God's presence before I could even get home.

When I finally got home, I raced into the house to pack a different suitcase in preparation for making the six-hour trip to Houston. My husband, Bob, was not in a hurry to get in the car and make the trip because he did not realize how serious the situation was. That only lasted until David called again. This time David told us that the doctors had said, "Genevieve was the sickest pregnant woman in the whole Houston medical center." Needless to say, we made the trip to Houston in record time.

Initially, we were told that there were three blood clots, two in one lung and one in the other. Immediately, the doctors began treatment to stabilize and dissolve the clots. By the next day after further tests, the doctors told us that Genevieve had a total of five blood clots. Five! Three were totally blocking one lung, and two were in the other lung leaving a small pathway. Every breath was a struggle for Genevieve, and she was exhausted. Her mom and I could only sit quietly with her because talking made her breathing even worse. It was a very long day and much of a long night.

But, oh the power of all those prayers! God's grace and mercy fell upon Genevieve during those uncertain days and long hours. By day three, there was a remarkable change in her breathing pattern. While not normal, she was not having nearly the struggle she had during the days before. She was able to leave ICU on day four, and each day thereafter God's healing hand was upon her. So much so, that by the end of one week, she was able to go home! This was almost unheard of! Prayers of thanksgiving rose to heaven for God's healing miracle.

In truth, Genevieve should not have survived. Her condition was so dire that an emergency C-Section surgical cart and a baby-warming unit were parked outside her room at all times. It even followed her from ICU to her room on the regular floor! It was always there so that if the unthinkable happened the doctors would try to save baby Connor even though he would be born very prematurely. Our family could have so easily lost one or both of them. Thankfully, God intervened. He pulled Genevieve back from that cliff and protected Connor until he could be born safely.

For various medical reasons, the doctors did not want the pregnancy to go full term. So, Connor Adam made his debut three weeks early on December 1st, 2015. Connor is a happy, healthy baby and shows no adverse effects from all the trauma his mommy endured that week. Genevieve also has returned to full health with no further medication or treatment required. Thank you, God!

When I tell people about what happened, they get cautious looks on their faces because they expect a bad ending. Praise God that is not the ending I have to tell. After hearing this story, a nurse told me, "Just step back and be amazed at God's miraculous work!" And I am amazed! My whole family is amazed and so thankful because what God did. He worked a miracle.

Travel Mercies

Judy Burton

*M*y name is Judy and my story starts in 2002. My husband and I moved to Wyoming in the fall of 2001 so the following year began what would be numerous trips back to Oklahoma for us; some trips would be together and some individually for each of us. Between bad weather, heavy road traffic, and the relentless pull to be back home for various events we were continually on that drive. We started out those first three to four years with seven to eight trips a year. Then when my husband's job kept him in Wyoming more, three to four trips a year with me taking two to three by myself. The average of 2900 miles a trip was not uncommon and would more times than not be closer to 3200 miles.

I had never heard of anyone saying a prayer for travel mercies and thought it odd the first time I witnessed it. I thought "what a strange idea", how little did I know that no matter what it is called – Safe travels to you; Hope you get there safe; May God watch over you; God speed; etc., travel mercies are real. Travel Mercies have become something I pray for. We have no guarantees in life.

My first experience with how I came to ask for travel mercies was on the road to Oklahoma in the spring of 2003. The roads in Wyoming were slick with patchy ice and high winds most of the way from the northern part of the state to the southern border. I left home around 6:00am that morning and before I drove two hours south I was starting to really get into some black ice conditions and that incessant wind. I passed a tour bus that had turned over into the median and also a semi-truck and trailer.

By the time I had gone four hours, I was in the biggest mess of a storm I'd ever been in. I topped a hill with about a half dozen other vehicles and my car hit a patch of ice and I was headed for the ditch. I cried out in terror to the Lord to take control – I couldn't do it alone. I closed my eyes and gave up, paralyzed with fear of what was about to happen. The Lord heard my cry and took control! I opened my eyes and I was still on the highway, out of the jam that had moments before been unavoidable. The Lord says that if you call out to him, he will hear you. In Psalm 34 the Bible says, *"I sought the Lord, and he heard me, and delivered me from all my fears"*.

May of 2005 once again found me on the road by myself headed to Oklahoma. The trip down was uneventful and the visit with the new grandbaby priceless. The return trip was riddled with anxiety. It all started with wave after wave of severe thunderstorms that had hail and tornadic tendencies. I thought I could dodge around some of the most severe by taking various roads more west than north and found myself in Colorado. [I love how the radio announcers always give weather bulletins by the various counties that are in the path of the storm. I don't know how some people are that travel, but I don't travel from county to county with the names in my head and especially in foreign state]. The sky was a very dark ominous green/gray color, the wind was howling, and I was the only car for miles. The weather bulletin came across the radio, "County X take cover now. If you live in county X seek shelter immediately – Tornado on the ground!" My first thoughts were, "I am driving where? Am I in this county somewhere? There is an overpass up ahead. I stop under it and pull out the map. County X, ok got it, yeah, I am in county X, now what? Do I sit here and wait to see what is going to happen or do I drive on?" The radio names two towns that I look at on the map. A road sign I just passed before stopping named that town to be five miles from here. The other town was ten miles in the rear view mirror. I felt like a sitting duck with a target on my back. It had started to hail and the wind got even more severe. There was a wall cloud covering the whole sky to the west of me. I was sick with anxiety and fear. I prayed. I prayed like I hadn't prayed in a long time, "Oh Lord be with me now". I sat there and prayed through the storm. For twenty minutes or more, I just closed my eyes and prayed. I had never heard a roar like that. The tornado went through the town in front of me, as well as, the town behind me. It hit both of them. I had one ding in the hood of my vehicle from a hailstone that bounced off the highway.

I was safe because the Lord was watching over me. Hebrews 4:16 says, *"Let us therefore come boldly unto the throne of grace, that we may obtain mercy, and find grace to help in time of need".* I believe. I believe in God and I believe in His Word.

I have been through other situations while traveling the roads to Oklahoma. I always end up relying on the Lord to get me through. There is no person and no situation that the Lord cannot handle. The answer is so simple. Just ask. Just ask the Lord for travel mercies. Whether it is a physical road, an emotional road, or a metaphoric road that you find yourself on, ask God and He will be there.

Healing

Mary Beth Bruce

*M*y name is Mary Beth and I have two boys named Kaegan and Karter. Kaegan was a normal kid who ate everything in sight and especially loved sweet treats. He was excited to be a big brother, and then we got fussy Karter! Karter cried a lot and was just never happy. It wasn't until he was 2 ½ years that we found an awesome nutritionist. We had been through every doctor's test they could think of and it showed nothing to be wrong. He was having asthma attacks every night that were gradually getting worse. He was on a $300 worth of meds a month, two inhalers, two allergy meds and a reflux medication. He was a very miserable little boy. The nutritionist's test showed he had 20 different food intolerances. She put him on a very special diet of zero preservatives and none of the foods he showed an intolerance too. Within two weeks, he was a changed boy! He was happy and gaining weight!

February 6th, Kaegan got sick. He couldn't keep anything down and just lay around. We were in and out of the hospital and they found nothing. On the 17th, I took him to a pediatrician in Frisco, TX. They drew blood labs for food allergies. It turned out that he had a corn allergy, a wheat allergy, and celiac. I was so very overwhelmed with all of these food restrictions, but we made it work and both boys were doing better. Life with that many food restrictions is hard and isolating. Normal things that most wouldn't think twice about were stressful. Spending the night with friends was impossible. But God!

July came around and Kaegan was envious of kids going to church camp. He wasn't old enough to go, but I remember warning him I wasn't even sure it was a possibility for him. He couldn't even eat food that had been cooked in a pan that

11

had ever had gluten in it. He looked at me and said with the true conviction and faith of a child, "God is going to heal me and I will go to camp and not worry about a thing. And God is going to heal my brother, too!"

Almost a year passed and I was starting to worry. I was checking with the camp sponsors and cooks to see what sending food to camp would entail. I could pack his food and label it and he would get it from the nurse. Stress!!! We had switched pediatricians though and they wanted Karter to see a GI specialist again. A week before his appointment, I had a dream. Kaegan always corrects me and says it was a vision. When I woke up I just knew I could feed them whatever I wanted because they were healed! We decided to wait and see what the doctor said. It turns out he didn't like any of the tests that were performed on either kid and wasn't convinced they were ever sick. I know that they were two very sick little boys though! I had seen the results of changing their diets on their lives! He wanted them off their diets, which I was fine with because God had prepared me through the dream. Week one, we did just one normal waffle a day. Week two, we did two normal waffles a day. Week three, they ate everything they could think of! My boys were healed! Kaegan went to kids camp and his pastor sent me pictures of him with food piled high on his plate! God can do absolutely anything!! Kaegan ate so much at camp he gained two pounds that week!

An Angel to Watch over Me

Kay Schutte Bryan

My husband, S.J. and I had driven to Houston for our grandson's graduation from high school. We had some late nights visiting with family and friends, but Monday morning, June 6, 2016, we headed for home. Generally, with stopping for lunch, it is an 11-hour trip to Hobbs, New Mexico. About 8 miles south of Big Lake, Texas, around 5 PM, I was sleeping. S.J. had the cruise set on 75, which was the speed limit at that time. He drifted off to sleep until the side rug-board highway and gravel spewing, woke him. I was awakened by his screaming, "Oh My Gosh!" Frighteningly startled, he was hurtling off the highway. He overcorrected and flew across a two-lane highway. We vaulted off the road, rolling three or four times before smashing into and splitting a tree. We rolled again and stopped upright. I knew what was happening the whole time and kept wondering if we were ever going to stop rolling. A Yeti cooler glass flew into S.J.'s forehead starting a flow of blood cascading down his face like a waterfall. I was fully alert. I wiggled my foot assuring myself that I was not paralyzed.

I grabbed my cell phone from my pocket and dialed 911. I was extremely weak; both hearing aides had shot into the air, so I couldn't hear if anyone answered 911. I looked at my cell phone that said "emergency response alert." I did not know if anyone answered. I was afraid my battery would run down, so I turned it off after a while. I kept wondering why no one came. S.J., knocked out by the Yeti cup, stared in a dazed shock. I asked him if he was hurting anywhere really bad. I told him that blood was rolling down his face. "Where are the paper towels?" I asked. He answered, "In the back seat." I was able to reach back and grab them. Tearing several off, I handed them to him. "Try to hold them on your face where the blood is coming from to stop the flow," I said.

Suddenly a man appeared on my side and asked how I was. I was so thrilled that help was there, I exclaimed, "Thank God, someone finally came!" I told him that I thought I was okay. My chest hurt, which I figured came from the seat belt. My lower back hurt badly, cramping whenever I moved. I figured it was from the seat belt also. The man moved around to S.J.'s side and constantly reassured us, "Everything will be okay and help is on the way. They will be here soon."

"How do you know that they are on the way? Did you dial 911?" I questioned. "I dialed 911, but I wasn't sure if they received the call," I continued. He did not answer my query about his dialing 911, but just kept telling us that we were going to be all right and help was on the way. "Would you undo S.J.'s seat belt?" "No," he replied, "You do not want to do that. He might injure himself. Help is coming. Be calm." Then, he was on my side of the car again, and he quietly said, "I'm just going to tell you, 'Good Bye' now. Help is here. You are going to be okay."

Racing through my mind was the thought, "Why are you leaving just when someone else came to help?" but then the trooper opened my door and asked how I was. I told him I thought I was okay but just really sore all over. I had no idea that I had broken my lower back and had a compression fracture of C1 and C2. He put a neck brace on me as a precaution. At my request they moved my legs carefully outside the car, so I could stand up to get onto the board to put me in the ambulance. They were working with S.J., preparing him for an air ambulance to San Angelo Shannon hospital, a level two trauma center.

They took me to Big Lake hospital in the ambulance. They helped me call my daughter on my cell phone. I told her that her dad was on the way to San Angelo and I was going to Big Lake. I told her I thought I was okay, but her dad was bleeding profusely and I was worried about him.

My daughter, Tonia, headed for San Angelo from her home in Odessa, Texas. Meanwhile, after examining me, they discovered my broken back and neck and took me to San Angelo also. The next day, the troopers came to the hospital in San Angelo to check on S.J. and me. My daughter asked them if they got the name and number of the man that had stopped to help her parents. She wanted to let him know how we were and thank him for stopping.

The troopers said, "There was no man there, Ma'am, we were the first ones on the scene." Then I knew that the man was an angel and they could not see him there telling me goodbye.

Saving Grace

Savannah Carr

From a young age, God has made himself known in my life. From me seeing angels as a child to Him performing miracles throughout my life. At the age of 14, I was diagnosed with a giant cell tumor that was eating away at the bone in the ball joint and socket of my left hip. I was very active with soccer and track so this was devastating news. Especially, hearing the possibility of losing my leg if the biopsy results confirmed cancer. That night, for the first time in my life, I grabbed a Bible and got on my hands and knees crying out to God. I began reciting scripture I didn't understand, to a God I had never known. He heard my plea and told me He'd take care of me. I was going to be okay. No cancer.

The doctors called the next morning with my test results and I was cancer free! I would need intensive surgery to remove the "Giant Cell Tumor" though. They used a cadaver bone and replaced my entire hip. I had to relearn walking and used crutches for a year. Although the doctors didn't think it was going to be possible, I was able to run and play soccer again.

After the birth of my two children, I struggled with depression and PTSD. I resorted to the common coping mechanism of drugs which had a long line of familiarity in my family. Bad choices, bottled with prescription medication, led to hard drugs. Since no amount of any substance was able to fill the void, I just kept digging a bigger and deeper hole. I did not know what reality was any longer or where the world of delusion and fantasy started. I destroyed what I loved and hurt all the people who loved me. I did unspeakable things to get what I wanted. I left my children, their father and my family to deal with the consequences of my drug use and lifestyle choices. Through everything, I can look back and see God's mighty hand of grace applied at just the right time in my life. He sustained me for HIS purpose. It was only when I met Jesus that I felt truly loved and fulfilled. He has shown me how to forgive myself and others. He has taught me how to become a loving mother, daughter, sister and a Proverbs 31 woman by His Word. After 9 months, I'm still learning a lot from the Lord and I'm so thankful for the Saving Grace Women's Home. I have had a tremendous amount of restoration with my family and my children. I am becoming such an amazing example for my kids to follow. Saving Grace saved my life. Now when I look back to my former days, I find it hard to believe that it was me who was in so much trouble. I'm certain that no physician in the world could have helped me and that no "psychopharmacology" would have healed me. But Jesus did through His mighty healing power. HE IS The Great Physician.

Failing to Listen

Robert W. Clay

It was a fall morning in October of 1991 and I was getting ready for an elk hunting trip to Colorado. I had made this trip many times through the years but this morning was going to be different. A friend that was supposed to go with me cancelled out at the last minute. I had everything ready to go – four horses, trailer hooked up, etc. Well, I had done this trip for so many years and there was just not any way I was going to miss out. The Holy Spirit spoke to me "Why don't you wait 'til later before you go?" I failed to listen to that small voice and instead let "self" rule the occasion. (My first warning from the Holy Spirit).

So I loaded up and took off not knowing what was down the road. I was at an intersection on Hwy 7 in Shawnee, Oklahoma when a DOT policeman put on his lights for me to pull over. I asked what was wrong and he told me I didn't have a tax sticker for my truck. I paid him on the spot for the fine and back on the road I went. (This was my second warning from the Holy Spirit). I continued on and arrived in Killeen, Texas where I stopped to pony my horses for a while. After about 30 minutes of exercising them, I loaded them back into the trailer and off we started. Going back onto the freeway was a steep grade and I saw a semi-truck coming from far back. As there were 2 lanes and I was gaining speed, I continued into the right lane. I noticed the semi coming up fast and I expected him to pull over into the left lane to pass. He came closer and closer. My first thought was "He is going to hit me!" That thought quickly turned to prayer for guidance on what to do. I heard the Holy Spirit speak to me saying, "When the truck hits, turn your wheels to the left". When the truck struck the

18

back of my trailer I did just that. The semi sheared off my fifth wheel hitch in the bed of my pickup, taking the trailer with the horses inside about 200 yards down the freeway before stopping. That semi was sitting up in the back of my horse trailer with four horses, crushed like sardines. My emotions told me to run and check on my animals, not knowing if I was hurt or not. Local ranchers heard the wreck and showed up in a hurry. They helped unload the horses and took them to a local vet. The horses were cut up pretty bad but still alive.

After all the excitement and inquiries by the Texas Highway Patrolman, he called me over to his car. He said the truck driver was asleep and would be in some serious trouble. He then took me to a motel, helped me get my truck checked out, and told me to stay there for a few days so he could keep a check on me. When I was ready to get back on the road, he offered me his new four-wheel drive truck to use on the rest of my trip. The local folks there were so nice. God puts good people in your path when you need them the most. I was so blessed to be alive. What I hope this story conveys to others is that God is good all the time. After God spared my life, I knew it was time to listen. So if He speaks to you in that silent or small voice and tells you "No", please listen and do what He says. If the answer is "No", don't do it. I'm grateful to have been spared on that day. I hope this helps someone down the road. Thanks.

Asking for Help

Linda Close

he doctor said my condition had been developing over several years and he wondered how I could have ignored the signs for so long. In looking back, I can see the signs now, but at the time I could not be deterred from doing the activities I wanted, or felt I was expected to do.

It was during the summer of 2015 that I first heard of Osteitis and I would soon find out how it would affect my life. After looking into why I was hurting and having trouble walking, standing, and especially sitting, I ended up at an orthopedic surgeon's office with an osteitis prognosis. I was told the only option for healing was a 14-18 month process consisting of nine months of non-use and transitioning into physical therapy to rehabilitate. At that point in time, I was in so much pain and it hurt to move. My body was tired of fighting to compensate for muscles that no longer listened to me. My healing process began with anti-inflammatory and muscle relaxant drugs and three weeks of flat-out bed rest. I slept a lot and was glad to be relieved of the worst pain. I then graduated to limited movement around the house and was spending most of my time in a recliner, reading, watching movies, and sleeping.

The soundest advice the doctor gave me was to warn me of the depression I would encounter and suggested that if I was a Bible reader to concentrate on the Book of Job. Depression did set in, as well as, feeling sorry for myself. I experienced many dark days wondering why I would want to live another day feeling as I did and living with the inability to do anything. Type A personalities aren't exactly exemplary models in the area of patience and I found the lack of mobility, isolation, and solitude, brutal. Job 7:3...*so I am allotted months of emptiness, and nights of misery are apportioned to me.*

I spent a lot of time asking God, "Why me and what are you trying to teach me?" During the darkest times, I would pray for some sign of hope or some glimpse that things would get better. On those days, I would get a call from a family member or friend to say they were thinking of me and I would know that I was not alone. I had one friend that called every afternoon to fill me in on community news and activities and I began to look to that call as a lifeline to a world of which I was no longer an active participant. She was my guardian angel. After about three months, I was able to ride, somewhat uncomfortably, in a car. My guardian angel would not only pick me up to take me to church, but she also knew that I would be unable to endure standing or sitting in the church pews for any length of time. She brought a padded lounge chair to church for me to use. My church family was happy for me to be back in attendance no matter what arrangements they needed to make. They all made me feel so welcomed and loved. I was truly blessed with other friends, as well. They were willing to drive me to church, to doctor appointments, and to help with chores, clean my house, and give their time for me. I was not good at asking for help. I know now this was one thing God was trying to teach me. It is ok for people to know that you need help.

In the fifth month, I was actually driving myself to the grocery store and was able to run a few errands. During the seventh month, the doctor agreed to let me begin some light physical therapy and I thanked the good Lord every day for the smallest improvements. I still do. During my tenth month of recovery, I was feeling great and had accomplished more than I had hoped for. Then my health took a turn and I required an emergency appendectomy. God truly blessed me because the doctor told me my appendix was gangrenous and would have burst had one more day passed. After being home for a couple of weeks and healing from surgery and a resulting hematoma, I was outside my home walking and enjoying the sunshine. I blacked out and fell, breaking my wrist and damaging some ribs. Just that quick, I was back to the recliner and learning pain control and patience all over again.

Along with the osteitis therapy, I am now including therapy for the healing wrist and ribs. My healing is not yet complete. I know I still have more months and more work to do. What I do know for sure is that God has been with me through this journey. I feel truly blessed by all the angels He sent my way, by His guidance to learn patience with myself, how to listen to my body, and to learn how to ask for help. I need God's help every day to show me His path.

For those of you who are feeling alone and isolated, have faith and trust in the Lord and He will provide the light during your darkest hours. **JOB 29: 2-3**..*As in the dawn when God watched over me; when his lamp shone over my head, and by his light I walked through darkness.*

In His Word Do I Hope

Chuck and Jan Darby

*P*salm 130:5, one of the "Songs of Ascents", states, *"I wait for the Lord, my soul does wait and In His word do I hope."* (NASB) Jan and I learned early in our walk of faith what it means to have our hope, our trust and our confident expectancy in the Lord and in His Word.

In 1982, I was on staff at a church in Arlington, Texas. In that same year Jan became pregnant with our first child. We began the exciting preparation for our child. We had bought our first home two years earlier. I remember Jan and I would go into our spare bedroom (soon to be our nursery) and visualize where the baby furniture would go. With each month of Jan's pregnancy, our excitement and anticipation grew. Jan had found an OB/GYN whose last name was Pickle. So began the regular scheduled visits with Dr. Pickle. He ordered a sonogram and we discovered that the Lord was blessing us with a son. Jan's pregnancy was very routine, if that is possible. All our doctor visits were good. We were planning, buying and moving things in and out of what would be a "bear" themed "boy blue" nursery.

As 1982 came to a close, our church traditionally had a watch-night service on New Years Eve and that year was no different. That year December 31 fell on a Friday. Earlier in that week, Jan went to her scheduled appointment and I was able to go with her. The best I can remember, the visit was short and sweet. Dr. Pickle said, "Everything is progressing on schedule and we are still talking about an April 1 delivery". So on Friday night, December 31, 1982 we joined with our church family to celebrate and to ask the Lord's blessing on the New Year, 1983. The worship service progressed leading to a time of prayer for the

New Year. It was during this time of prayer that our pastor turned to Jan and me and said, "The Spirit of the Lord says, the baby is fine and the pregnancy will be full term". I remember thinking to myself at that moment, "Wow, what spiritual insight" (very sarcastically). I am so thankful that the Lord has forgiven me for my sarcasm. In that moment it seemed to be information that was obvious and known. We had basically heard the same thing from the doctor. The new year, 1983, came just like every year before it and we never thought again about what the Spirit of the Lord had shared with us that night, until the first Friday in February.

Friday, February 4th, began like most of our mornings, as we were up early. I went to the church and Jan was getting ready to, of all things, substitute at the churches' Christian school. The morning progressed with both of us busy. Sometime during the morning, Jan noticed excessive swelling in her legs and feet. She took some time and called her mother and she suggested that she call her doctor. She found me and told me that she had called the doctor and they instructed her to come in so that she could be checked out. Jan left the church and drove a few blocks to the doctor's office. She told me she was fine to drive and that she would call me from the doctor's office. I told her that as soon as I could get a couple of things situated I would come to the doctor's office. Our church secretary came into my office and said, "Jan is on the phone". I could tell by the tone of the secretary's voice that there was reason for concern. I picked up the phone to talk to Jan. She was very emotional and said, "You need to come now because Dr. Pickle is admitting me into the hospital and is talking about taking the baby early". Before I left the church, the available staff had prayer with me. The church, the hospital and the doctor's office were all within blocks of one another. I was at the doctor's office within minutes. Jan was in a room on an exam table having her blood pressure monitored. I felt guilty for not driving Jan to the doctor's office myself but neither of us thought anything was out of the normal scope of the pregnancy. Dr. Pickle came in and began to give us his professional opinion of the situation. He said Jan was dealing with toxemia and that the baby was under extreme stress. He proceeded to lay out for us his progression of expectance, which included an early delivery and a pre-mature baby that would require special care at the Children's Hospital in Fort Worth.

He continued to assure us that we were in good hands because this was his area of specialty. So Jan was quickly admitted into the labor and delivery wing. We were already pre-registered for an April 1 delivery. Jan asked me to go home and get some personal items for her. We lived nearby, so while they were getting Jan settled into her room, I rushed to our house.

While driving the short distance to our house, I was trying to take all of this in. When I pulled up into our driveway I heard in my spirit the voice of our pastor saying, "The Spirit of the Lord says, the baby is fine and the pregnancy will be full term." That sure Word of the Lord came alive in my spirit and all fear and anxiety were dispelled. I could not wait to get back to Jan to remind her of what the Lord had said to us when this New Year began. I knew it was important to get back to the hospital so I could declare the Word of the Lord and change the atmosphere around Jan and our baby. I recognized that fear and uncertainty were trying to fortify themselves around us. We had pre-paid for our delivery with the hospital, but because of this early admittance and the possible extended care, we were asked to pay an additional sum of money. We did not have any insurance so this compounded the challenge of our faith, but the Lord is faithful in His provision. In going back to the house to get certain items for Jan, she had asked me to specifically bring "The Bible Promise Book", which was a gift from a dear friend of my mother's. We had not yet opened the book since it had been given to Jan a week earlier.

Dr. Pickle was very matter of fact and to the point. The problem was that his "to the point" approach was always worst-case scenario. I hurried back so I could remind Jan of what the Lord had said to us in the watch night service. When I got back, Jan's hospital room was filling up with nurses, aides, and family members. I had so wanted to get back to Jan with this sure Word of the Lord before this went much further. I wanted her to know that it was going to be all right, because the Lord has given us His sure Word and we could rest in Him. Dr. Pickle had managed to get into room before I got back and he laid out a series of expectancies on how this was to develop, all based on his experience and expertise in this particular area. It seemed like it took forever for me to get back to Jan to remind her what the Lord had said about the baby and her pregnancy. When I got to her bedside, I immediately declared the Word of the Lord to her and to our baby. I knew in that moment that she received those words of hope and assurance that her womb was filled with the confident expectancy of God's Word. Having our faith strengthened by His Word, we began to rest in Him in the midst of all the unrest around us. Sometime in all this Jan took the Bible Promise Book and opened it. In the book was a check that was more than enough to meet the amount the hospital said they needed from us. The Lord knows what we need before we need it. That was evident in the Word He gave us in the watch night service and the financial provision He made for us a week earlier than we needed. I continued to say "In His Word do I hope".

The doctor continued to come in throughout the day and he would say we would probably have to take the baby this evening. Jan and I would say to one another "the baby is fine and the pregnancy will be full term". They monitored Jan and baby Samuel all though the afternoon waiting for these certain indicators. Finally, as the day became night, Dr. Pickle made a statement that he would repeat almost every day from February 4th to March 28th, which was "I will probably have to take the baby tomorrow". Jan remained in the hospital through most of the weekend because her blood pressure remained at a very high level. On Sunday afternoon, Dr. Pickle said Jan could go home but she had to be pretty much confined to her bed, except to come to his office every day, Monday through Friday. On Saturday and Sunday she had to go to the hospital to be checked. When Dr. Pickle released Jan to go home, I told him, "the baby is fine and the pregnancy will be full term". His response was "Trust me, I have seen this happen too many times".

So we began our daily routine of going to the doctor's office at 8:00AM and on the weekends we would go to the hospital. They continued to monitor Jan and check the baby. The response was always the same each day; "I will probably have to take the baby tomorrow." We would respond by saying, "The baby is fine and the pregnancy will be full term". This went on until the morning of Tuesday, March 29, 1983 when Jan's water broke and shortly after she gave birth to our son, Samuel Luke. After the delivery I told Dr. Pickle, "thank you for taking so much time and care of Jan and Samuel". I also reminded him that the baby was fine and the pregnancy was within 3 days of the due date.

It was that Word of the Lord spoken to Jan and me in that watch night service that anchored our faith each day as we trusted and put our hope in Him and
His Word. Dr. Pickle said after the delivery that he would not have believed that
Jan would make full term because everything about her situation was textbook
for a pre-mature delivery. I declared to Dr. Pickle what was reaffirmed to Jan
and me everyday for almost 2 months, which is that our trust, our hope, our
faith in the Lord and His Word will never allow us to be disappointed. To God
be the glory for the great and wonderful things He has done for all of us. "And
in His Word do I hope". Psalms 130:5 (NASB)

Dad's Golden Chariot

Janet Sue Dean

*M*y story begins on Aug. 5, 2000. In the past ten years my dad had prostate cancer for which he went through a series of chemotherapy treatments, a heart attack, a serious infection when he had his open-heart surgery, and a stroke that he was still struggling with the side effects. He was a retired teacher but a farmer/rancher at heart. He had raised horses, mules, cows, chickens, guineas, goats, sheep, rabbits, turkeys, pigs and who knows what else. He was determined to still drive his tractor and brush-hog the pasture. Unfortunately, on one of those days, he got his tractor on top of a stump and broke the glass bowl on the fuel pump. We lived 70 miles from the hardware store where he could get the part for his tractor. He could no longer drive, and as one of six children, it became my turn to take him to Texarkana to get the part.

We left early with the intention of making a quick trip even though it always ended up as an all-day event. We went to the hardware store and picked up the part and then headed to Ashdown, Ark. where he got his haircuts. His friend Jo was his barber. Jo and her husband went on trail rides with Mom and Dad. We arrived at her shop and she called her husband who came and the stories began to roll. When Jo finished cutting Dad's hair, he turned to her and said "Jo, this is probably the last time you cut my hair". She just laughed and gave him a big hug as we left.

We returned to Texarkana and went to Tamale's for lunch. This was mom and Dads favorite place to eat. Even though Dad had taught children to read for years, because of the stroke I had read the menu for him on previous trips. Today he insisted on reading it and ordering the enchiladas by himself. Mom ordered her usual, chicken strips. We all enjoyed our meals and headed for home. Dad seldom asked to stop on the trip home but today he asked to get something to drink at DeKalb. Mom and I always stopped and that was our plan. On arriving at the Dairy Freeze, I drove into the drive- thru and then realized it was closed. On a Saturday afternoon? There is a restaurant with a drive-thru across the street and Dad agreed that would do. As we pulled across the street there was a pick-up parked in the way of the drive-thru. The driver, with his friend standing beside the driver's door, continued their long conversation. After finishing their visiting and moving on, we drove up to the window and ordered two waters and a tea. When I paid for it, I thought it was a little high but I just paid and waited for our drinks. They finally came, two teas and one water. Mom and Dad both insisted on water so the waitress graciously changed the tea to water and refigured my change. As we left the restaurant parking lot Dad spewed his mouthful of water and said, " This is awful".

As usual, on a hot summer day we had started the morning trip with mugs of ice water. I assured dad I could fix his problem and upon getting on the highway headed north I pulled over and poured out that awful Texas water and filled his cup of ice with good ole Broken Bow, OK water. He was very happy to have his ice water.

After crossing the Red River Bridge on HW 259, we approached a stretch of road construction and slowed and followed a lead car through the very short area under repair. I gradually increased my speed as we were approaching a sharp curve. As we neared the curve, we met an 18 wheeler loaded with a double layer of big round bales of wheat straw. Just before we met, I noticed that the top layer of bales was coming off the stack. I shouted to Mom just as one of those bales landed on the hood of my Windstar. The bale exploded and went over the roof of my vehicle, crushing in the windshield and front section of the roof. We found out later that the bales were not tied down and he lost seven in all. I turned to check on Dad and he asked, "What happened?" I told him we had a wreck. He had a gash in his forehead where the overhead console had come loose and hit him. He still had his seatbelt on, as did Mom and I. There was smoke coming from the dash and I told Mom and Dad we needed to get out of the car. I was terrified that it would catch on fire as we were covered with the straw and dust from the bales of hay. Mom unfastened her seatbelt and she opened her door and got out, clinging to the door to keep from sliding down a deep ditch beside the road. She reached the back door and helped Dad unfasten his seatbelt and get out of the car. He immediately began to slide down the ditch bank, which was covered with straw. The driver from the truck, which was following us, helped get Dad to the back of our car and laid him on the pavement. A man pulling a boat stopped and administered first aid to Dad. He was a medic and he "bagged" Dad to help him breathe. There was a family who was from Poteau that looked after Mom and got her in their car out of the August heat. Their son got in our car and talked to me to keep me calm and gave me water to drink. Dad began to call for Mom and she got out and went to him.

He wanted to know if she and I were ok. She assured him we were fine. The ambulance had been called and seemed to take forever to get there. While waiting, someone called my husband and they insisted that I talk to him so he would know I was ok. When I looked down after the crash, my right arm was resting on the armrest but my hand was hanging straight down with both bones sticking out a couple of inches. I grasped it in my left hand and pulled the flesh back down over the bones and squeezed it tightly to stop the bleeding. There was hair on the roof where it meets the windshield but I had no marks on my head. I had no red marks or bruising from the seat belt or air bag. God's hand leaves no bruises. I had no injuries except my broken arm and dislocated elbow. When the ambulance arrived, they attended to Dad, loaded him, and rushed him to the hospital in Idabel. They fought to save him but to no avail. His breastplate was weakened by open-heart surgery when he had his heart attack. The seatbelt had broken both sets of ribs and punctured both lungs. This sounds like a tragedy but with all he had been through and his anguish about his inability to live a normal life, it was truly a blessing. He begged us to promise him he would not have to go into a nursing home, which was a promise I could not make. I promised him I would do everything I could to prevent it. He had a blood clot described to be about two inches long that was flapping and just waiting to break loose any time and kill him or worse. He had lost his ability to read when he had his stroke. I worked with him and he learned to read again using the letters my brother Paul's wife, Jerri, and others had written to him.

He could read simple books but did not understand what they said. He could name all of his 6 children and tell everything about them and their families but he couldn't look at them and call them by name. He substituted words. He might ask for a hose but want the hammer. He was a wonderful husband, father, grandfather, great-grandfather and friend. He had taught for almost 40 years and was respected in the community. He was a leader in the First Methodist Church of Broken Bow. He was on the board and taught Sunday school class for many years. God had answered his and our prayers in such a way that he no longer had to suffer pain or fear tomorrow. Dad came to my brother in a vision before the funeral and told him " I am a teacher by profession, but a farmer by heart. This is some of the most beautiful farmland anywhere. Tell Sue those big round bales of wheat straw were my golden chariot. Don't be sad when she sees them." God is so good to those who believe, love, and serve him.

Mother was badly bruised by the seatbelt and had a cracked sternum. She healed completely after several months of pain. I had a double compound fracture of the right arm and a dislocated right elbow. I was transferred to the hospital in Paris, Texas. They spent hours getting the glass and straw out of my right arm. The wrist bones were splintered and an external bar was attached to my arm to allow my wrist to heal before they could pin my bones. After several weeks, surgery was performed on my arm and a shepherd's hook was inserted in one bone. The other bone was left untouched because of fear of infection. After leaving it in as long as possible, it was removed but my arm continued to swell and hurt. The pharmacist became concerned that I might have become addicted to the drugs, but I had not. When I returned for x-rays the surgeon discovered that my bones had separated where it was pinned and had overlapped. Fixing it would require more surgery and both ends of both bones would have to be cut off to permit healing and my right arm would become much shorter than the left. It was decided to allow nature to take its course. We know who nature is.

My husband had hip replacement at Bone and Joint in Oklahoma City. When he returned for a checkup, I felt I should get a second opinion. I got an idea my arm wasn't normally what they see when the tech asked, "How long has your arm looked like that?" Jerry's doctor spent his time looking at my problem and offered his opinion that was, "Just fuse it". The doctor, with whom I had the appointment, took one look at it and the x-rays and suggested that I see the hand specialist that had just joined the staff. I could see him after lunch because he was in surgery. Jerry and I went across the street and during lunch discussed the choices we had made right after the wreck. Should we have come to the city for surgery? After lunch we went back to his office, walked in and was taken back immediately to see him. He checked the x-rays and asked lots of questions. He then said, "Now, I will talk. This is the worst injury I have seen except one other, but he was young. With as good a use as you have, and the feeling is good, and the circulation is good, I would leave it alone. If we do surgery it might not help and could be worse. If surgery is needed in the future it could make it impossible. If I get a patient with a bad break, I'm going to send them to your surgeon." This did make me feel better about my surgeon but all the way home I still doubted my choices and when I went to bed I had a hard time going to sleep because I was still questioning my decisions. The next morning when I awoke I heard a voice say, " I thought you were going to let ME handle this. Two bones are better than one." There was no doubt in my mind that God had spoken to me, as there was no one else around. It was obvious to me who was speaking. I had an unexplainable peace about my arm and I no longer doubted my decisions.

When I taught Sunday School class and the book said to tell the children they would know when God talks to them, I questioned " how?" I no longer wonder. I have heard the voice of God! If the pinning had held I would have had one bone supporting my hand. As time has gone by, my arm solidified into one large bone just above my wrist and I can lift heavy objects and can use a small needle to sew and hand quilt. I have no pain. When my arms and legs were checked for nerve conductivity, three of them were good for my age (66), but guess which one was like that of a 25 yr. old? I told the tech " when God heals it, you don't have to worry about it. "

As I look back, I am amazed at the little things that happened to put my vehicle and the load of hay at the precise spot for the hay to fall on my hood from a truck I was meeting on the last sharp curve on HW 259 between Idabel and the Texas state line. The Dairy Freeze being closed, the driveway blocked across the street for the drive thru by visiting friends, incorrect filling of our order, returning corrected change, pulling over to pour out the nasty tasting water, following a lead car slowly thru the road repair area and slow acceleration for the upcoming curve, all played a major role in God's timing of the wreck. My sister was supposed to take him but she had a conflict of plans and I took him in my Windstar van rather than her small car. This could have changed the outcome tremendously. The fact that Mom and I had no life threatening injuries was by the grace and protection of God.

When someone notices my strange looking wrist, I have a testimony to share. I can tell about how God took care of me and my Mom and Dad during our wreck and how He healed my arm in such a way that it is stronger than the other arm. I can share how He strengthened my faith in a loving God who walks with us daily and is our strength in time of need, our joy in our hope of eternity. He is always there ready to listen and answer our prayers. Isaiah 59:1 "*Behold, the LORD's hand is not shortened, that it cannot save, and His ear heavy, that it cannot hear.*"

The Gift of Joy

Gerry Dodson

In the fall of 1964 I began experiencing some serious health issues. I would have a searing pain in my lower abdomen. I would faint and become cold and clammy. I was diagnosed as having cysts on my female organs. When a cyst would burst, I would go into shock. The doctor thought it was necessary for me to have surgery. On November 11, 1964, I had a hysterectomy. I did not have a fast recovery. I had three children in school and could barely take care of their needs. I dreaded facing each new day. By the time I took care of the basic needs of my home and family, I was exhausted. I had a recliner in front of a large picture window and would get my Bible and read all the promises on physical healing. I would meditate on what I had read.

Across the road from our house was a large pasture with lots of huge old oak trees. Since there were no leaves on at that time of year, the gnarled limbs were visible and looked dead. Everything in me seemed as dead as those limbs looked. Since I had so little strength, I spent most of my days in that chair reading my Bible. From November through late winter, I had no improvement. Then gradually, it seemed something in me was coming alive. I was regaining my strength and was able to take better care of my home and family. Spring finally came and I began to experience a joy I could not explain. I think God used His Word to heal me. That was 52 years ago. I am now 88 years old and I have not been in a hospital since, except for observation after a car accident.

The joy Jesus gave me has remained in my life in spite of the heartaches I have experienced. This should not surprise us for Jesus said, *"These things I have spoken unto you, that my joy might REMAIN in you and that your joy might be full"* John 15:11. **His promises never fail!!!**

Music from Heaven

Lillian Gibson's Story by Gerry Dodson

I know her as Lillian Gibson. She was born Lillian Harcrow in 1924, one of the few remaining members of the "greatest generation". Growing up in rural Oklahoma during the great depression, she learned many life skills that have served her well throughout her life. Her godly parents taught her about the love of Jesus and she accepted him as her Savior in her youth.

In 1943, she married William Gibson. They served the Lord together in the local church; always ready to volunteer when help was needed. Lillian baked cookies for the youth. She taught Sunday school and helped in Vacation Bible School. No one could make chicken and dumplings like Lillian. Her pan always went home empty after Church dinners. If friends or family were sick, she and William would show up with food.

Out of their union was born four children. One baby girl died after only 36 hours of life. They also lost one son, Hodge, when he was merely fifty years old. Their 57 years of marriage was filled with times of joy and times of sorrow. There was grief with their losses but they never lost their faith in God.

When William was diagnosed with cancer, Lillian sat with him in the hospital during his final days. She embroidered dishtowels to help pass the time and donated them to the church for the annual bazaar.

The day came when medical procedures could no longer sustain life for William. The family gathered for their final good-bye. As his earthly life was ebbing, he told his family of the beautiful music he was hearing. No one else could hear it. Some even checked up and down the halls to see if music was playing. Spiritual ears were hearing what physical ears could not. Apparently, the heavenly orchestra was playing a song to welcome William home.

God is Real

By Ferne Eu

A fall down a flight of steps resulted in back pain for many years. It was 1987 and I was residing in a boarding school in Belfast, N. Ireland. One morning while walking down a narrow, winding flight of steps, I somehow slipped. Before I knew it, I had fallen down the entire flight. I landed with searing pain throughout my lower back. Cautiously checking myself for further injury and seeing that I could move, I managed to get up and make my way back to my room. The next day I noticed a huge bruise on my lower lumbar region the size of a man's hand. Seemingly recovering from the fall, the bruise eventually faded away.

However, in subsequent months and years, I noticed that I would get lower back pain when I engaged in certain activities or took certain postures or positions. I could not stand for long without my back hurting. I could not bend over and in fact, any vigorous activity made it hurt. At the end of a long day it was excruciating to try and lie down. Hence, I started seeing a litany of doctors who could not figure out what was wrong with my back. X-rays did not give any indication of damage.

By 1992, the back pain was increasing in intensity. I was holding down a full-time job that required me to be on my feet all day. One Sunday evening I decided to attend the monthly Healing Service at my Church. After the minister preached his sermon, he prayed for all those who needed healing. He asked us to lay our hand on the part of our body that needed to be healed. I placed my hand on my sore back. The minister then prayed a prayer. I do not remember what he said only that I said "Amen". The minister asked for those that wanted to testify to God's goodness to come up and share their testimony. As I listened, I noticed something. That sore back that caused me great discomfort was no longer painful. I had no feeling of pain or discomfort at all. Did God heal me? Or was my imagination working over time?

I wiggled around in my seat testing out my back. I bent this way and that. I shrugged my shoulders, leaned forward and backward. No, there was no pain. And yes, God did heal me. By the time I realized the miracle God had performed for me, the minister had dismissed the congregation and everyone was preparing to leave. I ran forward and told the minister what had happened to me. To my astonishment and embarrassment he recalled the congregation to their seats. He told them I had a testimony. As I testified of my healing some elders came up to lay hands on me and pray. Before I knew what was happening, I was flat on the ground, enveloped by a strange warmth and light. Tears where streaming down my cheeks and I was overwhelmed by the sense of God's love and grace.

The next day after work, I decided to test my back again. I washed my clothes in the bathtub. A week prior doing this chore was done with much pain and discomfort. To my amazement, I was pain-free. In the following days I did other activities and still felt no pain. Neither did I go to bed with excruciating pain anymore after a long day at work.

I knew in my heart God was real, but this healing brought home to me how much He cares for and loves His children. I knew God healed but now I had a personal encounter with God, the Healer, himself. In these years that followed, I came to know God's character and heart in other ways, but I will forever remember the encounter with God because it was when He drew himself so near I could sense His warmth and light.

God's Faithfulness in the Ordinary

Anna Lester Evans

*S*haring a testimony has been a tricky thing for me throughout my life, mainly because I have been fortunate enough to lead a largely ordinary one. The trick lies in the notion that "testimonies" are dramatic stories, filled with divine intervention and radical transformation and "nick-of-time" miracles. What, then, is my testimony if I have been a believer in Christ all my life? When life feels mundane, what does God's grace look like? How do we encounter the divine in the everyday rhythms of work, home, church, school, and family time, again and again and again?

I suppose a snapshot of my walk with Christ at this moment in time is this: I am so thankful to find God's faithfulness in the ordinary. This lesson is one I'm still learning day after day. Whether intentionally or not, I internalized the message I and many others of a similar age were taught from camp speakers, mega-church pastors, prominent authors and other amplified voices for decades: That OUR PLATFORM is coming. It's practically a guarantee! The message goes a bit like this: God is willing and able to do great things in our lives. If we'll just be faithful to Him, He will exalt US as individuals as well! We'll know He loves us, because He will give us great influence and great book deals and great speaking engagements and great followings on social media, and we'll all be world changers and revolutionaries and top-tier conference speakers, if only we'll just love Him!

And the catch to this whole message, valid though it may be in some instances, is that obtaining OUR PLATFORM becomes the measure by which we know we are loved by God. It leads to a situation in which we're dissatisfied with the ordinary, because to walk with God is to experience the extraordinary by default. And if we're not constantly caught up in this state of supernatural providence, then…are we really being faithful? Are we really experiencing God? Are we really loved?

It's been two years and a few months since I graduated from college. In that time, I've gotten married, started my first professional job, and recently changed jobs to a new position I hope to hold for the foreseeable future. I am settling in. For now, many major life changes are behind me, and life looks pretty static for the next few years. What about the message I heard for so long? How does God reveal himself, if not through miracles and dramatic experiences and urgency?

I'm discovering how. I'm unlearning. I'm finding peace in the routine, quietly enjoying the goodness of everyday rhythms – paying bills, unloading the dishwasher, loving my husband well, doing high quality work, caring for the dogs and shopping for groceries and putting gas in the car, again and again and again. I'm cultivating faithfulness in these things, while learning and studying and seeking to know how God would have me do justice, love mercy, and walk humbly in the world around me right now.

I may not have a grand "testimony" in the way I've understood it for so long, but I'm thankful to God for a quiet season. I'm thankful for God's grace as life marches on.

I'm thankful to know He is with me at this time and at all times. I'm thankful for those who have gone before, quietly serving God whether anyone else knew about it or not. I'm thankful I don't have to prove my love for God before He shows His love to me – I would fall far short in that endeavor. I'm thankful that Jesus lived most of his life not as a popular miracle-worker, but as a faithful Jewish carpenter from Galilee. He knows about finding God's presence in the ordinary, too.

The Miracle of My Salvation

Tommie Garcia

My name is Tommie Garcia. I am the youngest of five daughters. I was the last to accept Jesus as my Savior. I won't go into a lot of detail but I was a broken child and a shattered adult woman. I spent a lot of my time trying to figure out how not to live for God and still not go to hell. I almost had myself completely brain washed into believing God might go Green. You know recycle humans-reincarnation.

Anyway, life had been extremely hard for me. I experienced life as an abused child and a battered woman. I had gotten past both of those issues but my brokenness was still within me. I had been married two times and divorced twice. My children had gotten to the teen years where I felt unwanted and unloved by their teen rebellion. I had an unfaithful boyfriend. I had reached a desperate place in my life where I really didn't want to live any more. I was on the verge of being suicidal.

I was heartbroken and crying when I went to bed on a Saturday night. I woke up at 1:30 AM feeling very lonely. Instead of calling my boyfriend who was one of the reasons I was down, I chose to go to the casino. I played the machines till 4 AM. I went home and went fast asleep. Sometime before 7 AM, I was dreaming. In my dream my youngest daughter, Sabra, and I were in a huge house the size of a small plaza.

There were some people chasing us. I told my daughter, "Let's hide in this small room". I could hear the men saying, "Oh, they think we can't find them in the little room". I told my daughter if we were going to survive we must get out of here.

Somehow, we got out and there were hundreds of thousands of people running so I started running too. There were these hidden doors under the street. You couldn't see them until you landed on them. The doors were beautiful like something you would see in a garden but you didn't see the door until it was too late. The doors would swing open and you would fall into hell.

I landed on a door. My door swung open and I dangled from it. I could see the people in the lava and fire screaming. I could even smell their flesh burning. They were all alive. Their skin was grey like those burnt from ash of a volcano. I was screaming, "God, this is too bad for anyone, even those who have committed unspeakable murders". I pulled myself up and begin to smash open doors so people would not have to go there. I also saw others dangling from their own doors. When I would touch their hand to pull them up, I could see the sin in their lives. I started telling God, "But that's not bad enough for hell" or I would tell God excuses for why they had committed that sin.

Sometime before 7:30 AM, my cell phone awakened me. I got up to use the restroom and turn my fan on because I was hot and sweaty. I fluffed my pillow and was getting ready to go back to sleep. I had turned my phone on silent. I heard a man's voice in my bedroom. He said, "REALLY, TOMMIE? ARE YOU GOING BACK TO BED AFTER JUST GETTING OUT OF HELL? DON'T YOU THINK IT IS TIME FOR A CHANGE? Isn't it time to tell the kids the truth and turn them around?" I jumped up, got my kids and went to church. I gave my life to God and this has been almost 3 years ago.

The dream I was given the next night explain the beauty of the doors and why hell was the appropriate punishment for sin. The door represents temptation. It is always presented as fun, and enticing like the gorgeous door. Before you land on the door it was a street but then you see beauty and hell. Sin doesn't show consequences until you open the door. This is how God explained it to me. When a man cheats on his wife you don't bring him a gift but instead you give him to his lover. When you don't serve God you serve Satan. When you go to hell you're just going to the lover of your choice. The way God explained it, I understood. I know I am supposed to be getting His message out there. He said to tell everyone that hell is near. This is my miracle and it has changed my life completely. I am no longer the same. Thank you for letting me share my miracle of salvation.

Our Unseen Guide

Rhonda Guthery

*P*arents of small children are accustomed to dealing with childhood illness; a cold, the flu, a stomach virus. The kind of ailment that usually last a few days; then the child is back to normal. My husband and I were the parents of three-year-old daughter and an eight-week-old son in March 2014 when our ordeal began.

Our daughter was sick, as good parents do – we took her to the doctor. She had a respiratory infection. Hoping to protect our baby from the illness we let her stay with her grandparents. It was Wednesday night, March 19th, when our son, Kollyn, became very ill. Thursday morning we took him to the doctor for wheezing. He was checked for RSV. The test was negative. We were sent home with instructions to watch him closely. All day Friday he seemed so sick. He could hardly nurse, his breathing was so shallow and in the evening he began vomiting. It lasted all night. Saturday we took him to an after hour's clinic. The examination revealed that he had an inner ear infection and a respiratory infection. He was given antibiotics and albuterol breathing treatments, with one being administered on site. His oxygen was low. Sunday showed no improvement in his condition. On Monday morning, we had another visit to the doctor. This time the lab test showed he tested positive for RSV. More antibiotics and breathing treatments were ordered. In the afternoon he was so sick we took him to the after hour's clinic again. He had now lost 10 ounces. The doctors advised us to take him to the Children's hospital in Little Rock, Arkansas. At this time he was so ill he passed out in my arms. I wasn't sure we would make it to the hospital.

We came to an intersection where we could go to Little Rock or to Dallas/ Ft. Worth. My husband said, "Google Top Children's Hospitals". All three of the closest hospitals were listed in – Little Rock, Dallas, and Ft. Worth. As Dallas was the closest to us, Dallas was it. But with the better of the two in Texas, the Children's Hospital in Ft. Worth was rated the best. That is how Cook Children's Hospital in Ft. Worth was where we landed in the ER that day. We were so scared for him. Not one police cruiser, red light, or road construction area slowed us down. Little did we know that our decision to go to Ft. Worth would save our son's life. We made a quick decision as to where to take him but I feel sure there was an unseen hand guiding us.

Our baby was admitted into the hospital and extensive testing began. The doctors tested him for Pyloric Stenosis, Meningitis, Flu, and RSV. The tests were negative except one – RSV was positive. The next day, March 24 he was moved to isolation and they were able to stabilize him. IV's for antibiotics and Pedi care were started with the antibiotic given every 30 minutes. He could not nurse or have any formula.

Once he was stabilized, the doctors began a food study and genetic work-up. He was finally able to have breast milk and was still on respiratory and IV support. Each day brought new challenges. The only thing we knew for sure at this point was he had RSV.

I had told my family not to put anything out on social media that we were out of town, but after a week of uncertainty and with no diagnosis still, I called my Mom and ask her to post a prayer request online. Prior to making that phone call, I had been online doing some research to see if there was any information about what we might be dealing with and thought I might have found a clue to what was going on. Then an uncanny thing happened while I was on the phone with my Mom. The nurse on duty had come in to insert a feeding tube into Kollyn. The nurse realized he needed something else from the supply room and as he was coming back into the room the desk nurse called him to wait, saying that the Geneticist had called and to hold off on the feeding tube and that she was on her way to see us. She came in and told my husband Jim and me that she thought she had found the answer to our baby being so sick. I told her I thought

I had found something online too. The Geneticist asked me to write down on paper what I had discovered online and she did the same thing with what she had found. We had both wrote down the same thing.

Our son ended up being diagnosed with Hereditary Fructose Intolerance (HFI). An indicator to this condition is Aldolase B deficiency in the lab tests. It is a very rare condition. Your body doesn't allow for any type of fructose, sucrose or sorbitol to be broken down and digested. At the time of Kollyn's diagnosis there were only five other Pediatric cases in the US.

Do you think it strange that at the very time I called Mom to ask for prayers is the time the answer came as to what was wrong? Jesus told his followers in Luke 18, *"Men ought always to pray, and not faint"*.

In the future day when Jesus rules over all the earth, he promises an immediate answer to prayer. *"And it shall come to pass, that before they call, I will answer and while they are yet speaking, I will hear"*. (Isaiah 65:24) I believe Jesus advanced that prophetic word and did that for our family.

There were so many tests to be made to verify what we assumed was wrong. On May 2nd we received the call that verified it. He did indeed have a genetic marker for HFI. Today Kollyn is doing well as long as we are careful about what he eats. He is an active two year old. When I look at him I am so grateful to my Heavenly Father for guiding us through the Valley of Death. There were so many times I thought we would lose him. Please never underestimate the power of prayer. It is the source of divine intervention in the storms that invade our lives.

She Looks Like a Little Angel

Cale and Misty Haley

*I*n April 2006, Misty and I went to Russia to get our daughter, Shalan. After a 12-hour flight from Atlanta to Moscow we arrived in the early morning hours. It was a gray overcast day and the people of Moscow were geared for a huge citywide celebration of "Victory Day" (a celebration of Russia's contribution to defeating Germany in World War II). A representative of the adoption agency met us at the airport. We were taken to our hotel and quickly dropped off. One of the first things that we tried to do was buy a sim card for our international cell phone. However, we quickly learned after walking about a mile from our hotel and to several cell phone stores we could not buy one because we were foreigners. As we walked back to the hotel, we both became very discouraged. Here we were halfway around the world on a rainy, gray day and unable to contact anyone from the agency about what we were supposed to do next. I started praying, "God, we need you to help us right now."

As I entered the lobby of our hotel, I heard a man reading a story to his daughter. I immediately approached him and said, "You're an American, aren't you?" Not only was he an American, he and his wife had just adopted a little girl. Also, to show you how wonderful God is, they were evangelical Christians from Southern California. They ministered to us and told us what to expect and prayed with us over the course of the next two days while we were in Moscow. A Christian couple from North Carolina also became a part of our group and they were about to go through the same process Misty and I were.

From then on everything fell into place. We figured out how to use the international phones in that country and the people from the agency were warm and friendly (all the Russians we met really liked Americans). From Moscow we flew four more hours to Kemerovo in Siberia. It was there, not too far from the Mongolian border, that we went to the orphanage to meet our daughter for the first time. If you can imagine one of the worst looking buildings in Broken Bow, this is what her orphanage looked like. Their playground equipment was old tires and broken swings and ancient slides. As soon as we saw the baby we fell in love with her.

The next two days flew by as we got to spend time with our daughter. We then had to fly back to Moscow and back to the United States. We were told by the agency that it might be up to a year before we could go back and get our daughter. While we were on the plane, the Holy Spirit spoke to me and told me so plainly, "Tell Misty that it will not be long before we can go back and get our daughter." I argued with God and said, "I'm not telling her that and getting her hopes up." The Holy Spirit was then adamant, "You tell her." So, I did. When I told Misty she turned to me and said, "I don't think it will be that long either."

It wasn't. We got a call in June and on July 4th we went to a courthouse in Kemerovo, Russia and were given custody of Evezenia Dandilova Tespota, who was renamed Shalan Faith Haley. Not only did the judge give us instant custody, she also waived the 10-day waiting period so we would not have to spend extra ten days in Russia. A couple of days later when we flew back into Moscow, one of the young ladies from the agency who was there to meet us was staring at Misty as she held Shalan. The young lady commented, "She looks like an angel." Misty and I just turned and looked at each other. This was significant because about a year before we left to go to Russia, a person at the church we were attending at the time came to us and told us that God had a word for us. He told us "You are going to bring an angel out of darkness." Know this, God is real and He loves you.

I have to share a story that the couple that we met from California told us to give more glory to God. A Christian couple from Louisiana had been given custody of their baby in Russia. However, their 10-day waiting period had not been waived. During that period one of the baby's relatives decided they wanted custody. The couple was heartbroken. The agency told them to stay in Moscow and they would try to convince the relatives to change their mind. The couple called their church at home to pray. After two weeks their credit cards maxed out and out of money, the heartbroken couple went to the airport to fly home. It is very expensive for foreigners in Russia. As they were about to board the plane, a representative from the agency came running to them with the baby in her arms. She told them the relatives had changed their mind and to take their baby home to America. Their prayers had been answered.

We're Walking Out of Here

Scott Hayes

On August 3, 2010, my wife, Patty and I were painting our two daughter's, Amanda and Autumn's room. The girls wanted to go play at a friend's house. We thought that would be a good idea. At 3:12 pm I get a phone call that no parent wants to receive. It was Autumn. She said Amanda was having a seizure. I hung up the phone and told Patty, "We have to go". Patty knew something was wrong. She said, "Is it the girls?" We got in the truck and she started praying. All I could say was, "Amanda". When we got to the friend's house, they were all in the backyard. I picked up Amanda and put her in the truck. We met the ambulance in the neighborhood. Patty rode in the ambulance and I followed. As a parent you want the lights and siren on. You want to get to the hospital as soon as possible. But there were no lights and no siren. We stopped at every red light in town. I was trying to stay calm.

When we get to the hospital, they give Amanda two rounds of valium. No change. The doctor wanted to give her some medicine for seizures, but they only had it in pill form. The doctor wanted to give her more valium and the pill for seizures. I told him we weren't going to give her more valium or try to force a pill down her. I told the doctor to find the medication in shot form and I would go get it if I had to. Patty wanted her to be transferred to OU or Little Rock.

The doctor found the medication at Paris. A hospital official and I drove to Paris to get the medicine. When we got back, they had Amanda ready to be airlifted to OU Children's Hospital in OKC. We had family, church family, and friends at the hospital. I don't even know how many people were there. They were gathered around praying for Amanda.

They put Amanda in the helicopter. I told Patty that we needed to go because we had a long drive, but Patty told me she had to see her take off. I wanted to leave, but we waited. When the helicopter took off, we started toward the truck but Becky Green intercepted us and said, "Let's go to the Idabel Airport". Becky had called Buck Hill to see if he would take us to OKC. He said he would if we paid for the fuel. Family, church family, and friends collected enough money to pay for the fuel and some extra for Patty and me because we had no money in our pockets. God will provide.

Buck and Mike Stauter flew us to OKC and drove us to the hospital. I can never repay them enough. When we got to the hospital, we weren't sure where to enter. We saw a helicopter landing so we went to that area. It was Amanda. We watched as they wheeled her off the helicopter and we followed them in and down the hallway. God told me two things in a loud voice, "Amanda is going to be okay and you all are going to walk out of here." I was too scared to look behind me so I looked at Patty and the two men who were wheeling Amanda down the hall. Nobody looked back. A calm went over me like I never had before. Later on when I talked about the voice, I had some people tell me it was just in my mind. It was not in my mind. It was God.

In my mind, I kept repeating to myself, "Amanda is going to be okay and you all are going to walk out of here." We got in the ICU room and I stayed up all night with Amanda. Patty slept for a couple of hours. We did a lot of praying and talking to Amanda even though she was in a coma. I kept thinking about what God had told me. I thought, "Amanda will wake up in the morning and the doctors will run some tests and we will be home in the evening." However, God doesn't work on my time frame.

The next day they ran tests, but Amanda did not wake up. OU Children's had a Ronald McDonald Room. Patty slept some during the night and I slept some during the day. We were able to have the room available for us the whole time we were there, even though it was originally booked for someone else. God provided.

Patty and I noticed that one side of Amanda was drawing up and the other side was not moving. Her feet were also tilting down. We exercised her feet, prayed, and talked to her. Family, church family, and friends came to do the same.

On the fourth night, Amanda finally woke up. We asked the doctor about brain damage. He never answered us but he told us we better get tough because there was going to be progress and setbacks. He was right about half of it — there was progress.

On the fifth day, Amanda was put in a regular room. Doctors wanted Amanda to walk as much as she could. They gave us a belt to put on her so that I could hold on to her when she walked. When we walked, Patty brought a wheelchair so when Amanda got tired she could ride. I literally jogged her down the halls. People thought we were crazy, but I didn't care. My girl was getting better.

OU Children's hospital had student doctors working with Amanda's regular doctors. One day one of the student doctors came into Amanda's room. He told us he had been following Amanda's case. He said when he read it, he knew the outcome was not going to be good. He said Amanda's recovery was a miracle. Patty and I told him, "God answers prayers."

On the eighth day, Amanda was released. I will never forget it. Amanda was lying in bed, wrapped in her green blanket. I asked her, "Do you want to walk out of the hospital or go for one final wheelchair ride?" Amanda looked me in the eyes and said, "We're walking out of here!" I had tears in my eyes. I knew it was God.

While we were in the hospital, I never told Amanda the two things God told me. I am glad to say Amanda is doing fine. When we arrived home, Amanda had cards from all over the United States. We are so thankful to *everyone* for their prayers and support. God answers prayers and He also provides.

A Chair for God

Sherry Holeman

*G*od is so faithful to His children and He loves to show His power to us in
ways that we could never imagine. Sometimes He gives us more than we
could ever imagine or dream.

When our son, Justin, was in his later years of college he decided to move
out of the dorms to save money and share an apartment with one of his college
friends. Justin called us one night and asked us to pray for him to find another
roommate. He said his roommate was moving out of the apartment so he would
need to find another place to live. He decided he would like to try to find a
house but would need to find something affordable or find another roommate
to share the cost. He asked us to pray for him that God would meet his need.

I was working at Little Dixie Home Health and had met Nadia, a little
Hispanic woman, who worked as an aide. I heard her speak with a coworker
about the power of prayer and that God can do anything. I wanted to share
Justin's need with her. God says in His Word in Matthew 18:19 NLT, *"I also
tell you this: If two of you agree here on earth concerning anything you ask, my Father in
heaven will do it for you."* I needed someone to agree with me for an answer for
Justin so I pulled her aside and said, "Nadia, please pray for our son to find an
apartment that he can afford. He needs to find another roommate to split the
rent with and can only afford $300.00 a month." She said, "Why you ask God
for $300.00? God is a BIG God and He can do ALL things! Why do you put
God in a box? He likes to do BIG things so you need to ask Him for free rent."
I thought I had faith in my life until I met Nadia but realized my faith was small
compared to hers. I am ashamed to say that I laughed at her that day just as

53

Sarah laughed when she heard the angel tell Abraham she would have a baby at the age of 90. I said, "Nadia I'm not asking God for free rent, just something Justin can afford." She looked at me and chuckled and said, "That's why you need to believe God for free rent because it's affordable. It will happen; you wait and see."

I barely knew Nadia so I really didn't know whether to take her serious. Every day for two weeks, she would come by the office to turn in her paperwork or pick up supplies. She would smile and say that she had been talking to God and He would soon give Justin free rent. I knew by the sound of her voice and the assurance on her face that she believed every word that she was saying. I would thank her and continue to pray that God would provide for Justin's needs. I prayed, "Lord, if your will is to give Justin free rent, then please do so."

On Memorial Day weekend, Justin called. He said he had some leads on a couple of rent houses but would not know for a few days. He asked us to continue to believe God to help him find the right place. We told him we would continue praying. He called again on Sunday afternoon to talk to us about his baseball game. After we talked a while, he told us he put a prayer request in at church that morning that God would provide him a house soon. Some of his friends were going to give him some leads on houses on Monday. He would know more after he talked to them.

On my first day back at work, Nadia came in and said, "IT'S COMING, Justin will have free rent soon!" I truly thought this woman must be a little crazy. Later that evening, Justin called and said, "Mom, I found a real nice house and it is very affordable." I said, "That is great, son!" He said, "Yeah, it is real great! You will not believe it Mom but the rent is …." I interrupted him and said, "Don't tell me it is free rent!" He said, "How did you know?" I said, "You are kidding me, aren't you? Is it really free?" Justin said, "Yes, Mom, it is free rent!" I was stunned and could hardly believe it. I asked Justin to explain. He said that one of his friend's parents was working as teachers in China and they needed someone to help their son take care of their house. He said his friend got permission from his parents for Justin to live with him in the house for free rent in exchange for him helping with the upkeep. They would only be responsible for the utility bill and part of the property taxes. I jumped out of my chair, did a little jig, and said, "I SERVE A BIG GOD!"

Justin wanted to know how I knew he would be getting a rent-free place to stay. I shared with him about my friend, Nadia, and her prayer for free rent for him. He was as stunned as I was that day. For two weeks I had heard my friend, Nadia, tell me that she was talking to God about Justin needing an affordable house. She said she wanted God to prove to my family and me that He can do anything. God had assured her that He would give Justin free rent. She had believed but I had doubted. I knew God could do anything but often do not have faith for my own needs. God truly proved to me that He could do anything.

I went to work the next day, with excitement in my heart, to tell Nadia of God's provision. She walked in the door, smiled very big and before I could say anything she said, "I told you God would give Justin free rent, didn't I?" She said, "Justin told you last night that God gave him free rent, did he not?" I said, "Nadia, how did you know that? Do you have a hot-line to heaven or something?" She said, "Sherry, when I talk to God in the morning, I pull up a chair while having my coffee and ask God to have a seat and share His goodness with me. We talk together and I read His Word and then we talk some more. I thank Him for all He has done for me then share with Him the needs that are on my heart. I tell Him to "show out" for everyone and prove the power of His might. Then I believe with all my heart that He has listened to me and heard my prayer so I start thanking Him for taking care of it." She said, "So many Christians put God in a little bitty box instead of opening the box and letting Him out to do BIG things for us. He said, *"We have not because we ask not"* (James 4:2-3)." She told me to take God at His Word and believe Him to do great things in my life.

Nadia and I have continued to pray for each other. I will never forget what God did for Justin that year. If you have a need in your life and are seeking an answer, then pull up a chair for God, spend some time with Him, and tell Him what you need. He wants His children to delight in Him so He can show us His power. *"Delight thyself in the Lord and He will give you the desires of your heart."* Psalms 37:4

A Phone Call

Sherry Holeman

God is such an amazing God that there are not enough words to fathom how He works in our lives.

My in-laws were wonderful people and we enjoyed them in our lives for many years. After a six-year battle with colon cancer, my mother-in-law, Mary "Gayle" Holeman died in July 2010. After Gayle's death, my father-in-law, Jack, went through some depression while living alone. He lived in McAlester, OK, which was two hours from us. Our children were very active so we didn't get to see him as much as we wanted but visited as often as we could.

In February 2011, Jack was scheduled for a small medical procedure. This started a progression of hospitalizations and surgeries for Jack that would last until November of that year. Jack was admitted into a skilled care unit in Norman after being diagnosed with stomach cancer. Randy, my husband, took off work and stayed with him day after day. Randy had such a love for his father. He told me that he and his brother had gone hunting with their dad on the week of Thanksgiving for 39 years in a row.

Every day, a minister friend would come by and visit and pray with Jack. There was such a peace in Jack's heart even though he knew things did not look good. Jack had recently given his heart to the Lord and was not afraid to die. In early November, Jack began a faster decline. It crushed me to see his health deteriorate so quickly but it also hurt me to see what my husband was going through. Many people took turns sitting with Jack but Randy did not want to leave his dad's side so he often slept at the hospital. Sylvia, Jack's sister, lived nearby and was very thoughtful and caring to us and made her home available to us. I would stay at Aunt Sylvia's house while Randy stayed at the hospital with his dad.

On Thanksgiving morning, Jack went to be with the Lord. He flew to heaven in the arms of his Savior. He was feasting at the banquet table with his wife, his mom and his dad. What a Thanksgiving morning for him! Knowing his suffering was over helped us get through a difficult day.

We left the hospital and went to Aunt Sylvia's to get our things. Our sons, Justin and Nathan, lived in Moore, OK. Nathan had invited us to their house for Thanksgiving dinner. I think Nathan knew it would help us to all be together that day. He was engaged, at the time, to a wonderful girl, Megan Latham. She and her mom, DeAnn, had cooked a wonderful Thanksgiving meal for us and delivered it to Nathan. We decided to join them.

About 11:45 a.m., I told Randy that we had better get on the road so Nathan and Megan wouldn't be waiting for us. We left Sylvia's and headed to Moore. Randy was driving dad's car and I was following him in our vehicle. I have no sense of direction so I knew I had to stay close to Randy to keep from being lost. As I was leaving Norman, I decided to call my sister, Tommie, to let her know that my father-in-law had died. She would be cooking Thanksgiving dinner at her house for our father. I rarely called Tommie on her house phone. She was taking college classes and was always busy so I knew the only way to reach her, usually, was to call her cell phone. However, I knew since she was cooking lunch she would probably be more likely to answer her home phone. When I hit the call button, someone answered the phone that sounded like my nephew, Junior. I said, "Hey Junior, this is Aunt Sherry. I need to talk to your mom." He said, "Huh?", so I told him again that I needed to talk to my sister, Tommie. He still acted like he didn't know what I was talking about so I told him my father-in-law had died and I needed to talk to my sister. He said, "Ma'am, I'm not Junior." My sister wasn't married at the time so I thought she must have had a boyfriend with her so I said, "Sir, can I talk to my sister, Tommie?" He said, "Ma'am, I think you have the wrong number." I apologized to him and was about to hang up the phone when he said, "I hope you find your sister, Tommie." He repeated, "I really hope you find your sister because I don't want you to be all alone on Thanksgiving. It is a terrible thing to be all alone, like I am. No one cares about me and I am all alone and it is a terrible, terrible feeling." My heart began to sink, thinking about the desperation this man felt so I asked him not to hang up. I told him he was not alone like he thought he was. I shared the verse in Hebrews 13 where God says, *"Never Will I Leave Thee or Forsake Thee! I Will Be with Thee to the End."*, and in Psalm139 where it states, *"He saw him being formed in secret in his mother's womb and that he was awesome and wonderfully made."* He began to sob and said, "Why did you call me?" I told him I was trying to call my sister, Tommie. He said, "But why did you call her on this number?" I told him that this was the number I had for her in my phone. He started crying even harder and said, "OH GOD! OH GOD! PLEASE, PLEASE PRAY WITH ME! HELP ME FIND JESUS! PLEASE PRAY WITH ME SO I CAN GO TO HEAVEN!" I told him, "Yes, I will pray with you." I shared the gospel with him and asked him to pray the sinner's prayer with me. I knew God must have taken over the steering wheel of the car because I was not concentrating on driving but on leading this complete stranger to Christ Jesus. After praying, the man said, "Thank you, God, for writing my name down in the Lamb's Book of Life." I was laughing and rejoicing. He began praising God for redemption from his sins. He said to me, "Ma'am, isn't it great to know that your father-in-law watched God write my name down in the Lamb's Book of Life." I told him, "Yes, it is." I asked him, "Sir, have you known Christ sometime before in your life?" He stated, "Yes, as a young boy." He said, "I'm glad you called today because just yesterday, I asked God if He really cared about me, would He please send someone to let me know He loved me?" He then said, "Had you called this number tomorrow it would have been too late because I was getting ready to hang myself with a rope that I had already prepared when the phone rang." My heart was pounding and I could hardly breathe, knowing what had just taken place. God had used a phone call that was supposed to be my sister's phone number to save a stranger from the depths of Hell. He said, "I know now that God really does love me. Would you pray for me every day? My name is Dave Eastham, and I am an alcoholic and a heroin addict. I want to live for Jesus but it's so hard because of my addictions."

After we ate dinner that day and I had shared the story with Randy and Nathan, I called my sister, Tommie, on her cell phone to tell her what had happened. She said, "Sherry, I thought I gave you my new house number. I changed my home phone three years ago." I could not believe what she was saying. The reality hit me of God's amazing power that ultimately led to a stranger's salvation.

I stayed in contact with Dave for a few years but we eventually lost contact with one another. The last time I heard from him, he was working in a soup kitchen in a Spirit-filled church in Moore, OK and was going to Celebrate Recovery meetings. I know Jack will rejoice to know his death brought salvation to a stranger.

God is so amazing. We serve a big God and He will do anything to make sure that people know Him as their Lord and Savior. Randy and I have learned to never underestimate how God chooses to work in our lives or the miracles that He performs. Sometimes He uses strange things to make miracles happen. If you wonder if God loves you, just remember this story and please know that God loves you more than you can even imagine and He will do whatever He has to do in order for you to feel and know His love.

Faith of a Friend

Sherry Holeman

My husband, Randy Holeman, and I will have been married thirty-four years this December 31, 2016. God truly blessed me when He brought Randy into my life. After we were married a few years, we decided we would like to have children. At age of 23, I gave birth to our first son, Justin and at the age of 25, I gave birth to another son, Nathan. Life was great with the boys. We have so many wonderful memories of raising our two sons. As I got older though, my heart longed for a daughter. We decided when I was about 28 we wanted to have another child. I did not know why but I could not seem to get pregnant. I had hemorrhaged very badly with both of my sons during child-birth so there was a part of me that feared what might happen to me should I have another child. I prayed for five years to conceive but it seemed my prayers were in vain. One day as I was praying, I felt the Holy Spirit whisper to me that I needed to quit asking God for a baby and pray for someone in our church who had never given birth to a child. I began to pray for a woman in our church to get pregnant. Every time I wanted to pray for myself to conceive, I sacrificed my want on the altar and prayed for my friend, Carey, instead. I prayed ear-nestly for months that God would bless her with a healthy baby.

One day, I decided it was time for me to see the doctor to see if there was something wrong with me. After my examination, my gynecologist told me I had endometriosis so the chances of me getting pregnant again were very slim. The doctor decided that I needed to have surgery for the endometriosis so he scheduled it for November 5th. The laparoscopic surgery went well but the doctor told us that he could not get all endometriosis so he gave me a prescription for some medication that would help my body get rid of the part he could not get while in surgery. He told us that it is imperative that I did not get pregnant while taking the medication because one of the side effects was severe birth defects. After much discussion, Randy and I decided to wait until the holidays were over before I started the medication because most medications made me sick. I did not want to be sick throughout Thanksgiving, Christmas, and our wedding anniversary, which was New Year's Eve so we decided I would take the medication the first part of January. At this point in our lives, we decided another child must not be God's plan. I was almost 35 years old and our boys were 10 and 12 so to have another child now would probably not be the best choice to make. Yes, making that choice crushed me but I knew it was probably for the best. We did not want me to get pregnant accidentally, when I was in my 40's, so Randy said he would make an appointment in January to make certain that did not happen. Isn't it amazing after we have a death of a dream and completely give up our plans that God takes our broken dreams and makes something beautiful out of the ashes? I had come to a time in my life where everything was out of my control and I could not fix this issue. God had showed me that this was something that only He could do and it was time for me to put everything in His hands so He could get started working it out for my good (Romans 8:28)

We celebrated Thanksgiving and Christmas with our families and then celebrated our anniversary at Queen Wilhelmina Lodge in Arkansas. In the middle of January, I was not feeling well so I made a doctor's appointment to see what was wrong with me. The doctor thought I might have a UTI and wanted to run some tests on me. A few minutes later, he called me back to his office and told me that the tests showed that I was 2 weeks pregnant. I could not believe it! I had just given up on my dreams of having another child and here I was pregnant again at the age of 34. I left the doctor's office that day wondering how I would tell Randy and the kids. That night I sat down with Randy and told him that I had gone to the doctor and the tests showed that I was 2 weeks pregnant. He was a little shocked, to say the least, but he was very happy. The next day we told our boys that mama was going to have a baby. They both gave me a puzzled look, then the oldest, Justin, put his hands on his hips and said, "Mama, are we adopting a baby?" I told him "No, we were not adopting." He asked, "Don't you think you are a little too old to be having a baby?" I told him I guess I was not because God had blessed us and it looked like we would be having a baby in September. He just shook his head and walked away and Nathan looked at me and said, "Well, it is time we have a sister!" I told him I was hoping for one but it would be up to God to decide what He gave me.

I had told my neighbor, Ginger, that I was pregnant and I would appreciate it if she would keep me in prayer. I told her I was not sure if I was ready to have another baby because the boys were in their middle school years and could now take care of themselves. She told me she would be praying for me. Part of me wanted the baby so much but then I began to think that maybe my son was right. "Maybe I should not be having another child. Maybe I am too old to have a baby. What if something major goes wrong this time?", I reasoned. I had so many questions but kept them deep in my heart so no one would know I had a lot of anxiety about the pregnancy.

In early February 1997, I got up one morning not feeling very well. I went to work and began my housecleaning duties. I went upstairs to vacuum the floors and as I lifted the vacuum up the stairs, something did not feel right. I decided I should sit down for a minute or two. After a few minutes, I got up and continued cleaning. After I got off work, I stopped at the grocery store to pick up a few things for supper and then headed home. After I arrived home, I put away the groceries and cooked supper. I told Randy I was not feeling well but I was not sure what was wrong with me. In the middle of the night, I awoke with major abdominal cramping. I got up to use the restroom. I knew something was terribly wrong. I soon realized I was hemorrhaging so I woke Randy to tell him to call the doctor. The doctor told me to elevate my legs and to come in to have an ultrasound. After the doctor's exam, he told me everything was fine with the baby but it was very important to stay off my feet for a while if I wanted to keep the baby. Due to my age and my medical history, I would need to be bedfast for 2 months. Randy took me home and prepared to be off work for a while to care for me.

During the time I was on bed rest, I became closer to God. I wanted the baby so much I would do whatever He required of me. He asked me to let go of some things I was holding on to that were hindering me from getting closer to Him. I made a complete surrender during that time. I had heard that music therapy helped when the body needed healing so I began to play a healing hymn praise music CD every day. I would lie the speaker on my belly in hopes that my baby would take hold of what the words were saying. I played one song repeatedly that said, "I am the God that healeth thee, I am the God your Father, I sent my Word to heal your disease, and I am the God your Healer." Every day my baby heard God's word in music form to bring healing and restoration.

Early one morning, I woke up in pain and started bleeding heavily. I told Randy something was wrong. I had done everything I knew to do and followed the doctor's orders but my body was not responding. I was in the process of having a miscarriage and I could do nothing about it. Randy began to pray for me but no matter how hard we prayed nothing seemed to help. I was laying on the couch in our living room and Randy was washing the dishes that morning when our phone rang. It was my neighbor, Ginger. She called to ask if she could come and visit me for a while. She said she had a gift for the baby and wanted to give it to me. I told Ginger I appreciated her thoughtfulness but my body was trying to abort the baby and I would probably have a miscarriage that day so I would not need it. She told me she was sorry to hear that and she would be praying for me. A few minutes later, I saw Ginger coming up our porch steps and knock on our door. I was dreading her coming in because I was afraid I would emotionally fall apart. Randy reassured me and then went to the door and asked her to come in. Ginger had the wrapped baby gift and told me she was not there to be cruel to me. She said she had bought the gift about two weeks prior but the Holy Spirit would not let her give it to me at that time. She said after our earlier phone call, she began to pray for healing to come to the baby and me. As she was praying, the Holy Spirit spoke and told her that now was the time to bring the gift to me. She did not want to upset me but she must be obedient to the Holy Spirit. She said the Holy Spirit told her that I was weak in my faith and she was to be my faith for me. She said I needed something tangible to hang on to while believing God for the healing. The baby blanket was God bringing something tangible to me to increase my faith. She said I had lost my faith because all I could see was the circumstance. Ginger spoke with authority that the Holy Spirit had assured her that God had heard my prayer and He would intervene and bring healing. Randy and I were both crying that morning as she was sharing with us.

I opened that gift and it was a baby blanket and three little onesies. She told me to lay the blanket over my belly and she began to pray in faith for the healing to take place. I barely knew Ginger, at that time, but on that day she was no longer just my neighbor but also my faithful friend. The presence of God in that room was so real that Randy and I could feel angels all around us. A peace swept over us. I will never forget that day. Even now, when I talk about it I can still feel the anointing that she had that day. Ginger told me that the enemy would try to convince me that my prayers had not been heard but when that happened I was to take hold of the baby blanket and remind him of what God had done that morning through the power of prayer.

Later that evening, the cramping and bleeding began to ease up. The following morning, the bleeding had stopped. I thanked God for it and believed God had healed the baby and me. In early March, I began spotting and cramping again. I called Ginger that day to ask her to pray for me and she reminded me of what she had told me about the enemy trying to convince me that God had not heard my prayer. She told me to lay the blanket across my belly and thank God for the healing, then remind Satan what God had done for me that day. I was obedient to everything Ginger told me. I held on to that blanket as Randy and I prayed and thanked God for healing. Later that evening the bleeding stopped and I began to feel better. Off and on throughout the pregnancy, my faith took a beating. Why was I like doubting Thomas? I would hang on to that blanket and pray with all my heart but there was a part of me that was so afraid that my prayers, hopes, and dreams would be crushed. I wanted to be strong in my faith as Ginger was but God had to work on me. Ginger was such a mature Christian. She was a prayer warrior but in order for her to be that, she had to fight many spiritual battles. My mother was like Ginger. Both of these women knew how to touch the hand of God in the midst of the battle. I wanted to be like both of them but in order to be that kind of warrior, God chose to put me in a place where I could do nothing but trust Him to see me through.

God was working on me in many ways throughout the pregnancy. I am proud to say that through much prayer and the faith of a friend, I gave birth on September 16, 1997 to a beautiful baby girl, Laura Michelle. She was absolutely beautiful and completely healthy. God had heard my prayers and fulfilled my hopes and dreams of having a daughter. Laura celebrated her 19th birthday this year. She loves music and has a beautiful voice. We enrolled Laura at Evangel University in Springfield, Missouri, where she is majoring in Music Education. She hopes to someday teach high school choir and work with youth ministry wherever God leads her. Laura calls Ginger her Godmother. She has a special attachment to her because she knows that she is alive today because of Ginger's obedience and prayers. I pray that everyone that reads this story will allow God to increase their faith in whatever they believe God to do. God also gave my friend, Carey, a beautiful baby girl, a year after Laura was born.

God is a miracle working God but sometimes He allows us to be put in places where all we can do is trust and obey Him. God is faithful and will do exceedingly abundantly above all that we can ask or think of when we put our trust in Him. God wants to fulfill our hopes and dreams but we must not waiver in our faith as I did. We must put our complete trust in Him to see us through no matter what the circumstance looks like. *"Faith is the substance of things hoped for the evidence of things we cannot see."* Hebrews 11

The Saved Microwave

Sherry Holeman

*O*ur daughter, Laura Holeman, has a call of God on her life and felt called by God to attend Evangel University in Springfield, Missouri to major in Music Education and minor in Youth Ministry. I told her that Evangel was a very expensive university but if God wanted her to attend there then He would provide everything for her.

Laura graduated from Broken Bow High School in May 2016 and right away we knew that the summer months would fly by so we started looking for everything she would need for college dorm life. I told Laura we still had her brother's dorm refrigerator but she would need to contact her roommate to see if she would provide a microwave. Laura contacted her roommate, Sarah, but she didn't have a microwave so we would need to find one. The search began for the perfect small microwave. I found an affordable one at Wal-Mart but a coworker discouraged me from buying it. She said it didn't heat food well so I began to search again. I looked at JC Penney's, Sears, Tuesdays, flea markets, yard sales, and the list went on. I decided to look on the McCurtain County Online Yard Sale for a microwave. I looked every day and almost every hour but never found one. I had told myself that my limit was $35.

We were visiting our sons on Father's Day when Nathan asked us what we still needed for Laura's college list. I told him we had everything but a small microwave. I had looked everywhere but couldn't find one under $35.00. Nathan told me to search Amazon and buy one from them. I told him I would look when I got home but that I had come to the place that I was believing God to provide Laura a microwave, not knowing where or how we would find it.

That evening as I was praying for us to find a microwave, God reminded me of a scripture I learned at age 9 in Philippians 4:19, *"But My God Shall Supply All Your Needs According to His Riches in Glory by Christ Jesus!"* There it was as plain as day, Christ Jesus would be providing Laura's microwave. He knew where one was and He would bring it to her in His time. I ended my prayer, thanking God for the microwave.

I try to pray every day as I head to work. The next morning as I was driving to work, giving God praise for all He had done for me, I told Him that I didn't know how or where the microwave would come from but I believed that He would provide. I reminded God of Philippians 4:19 and told Him to hold true to His Word and do not let my faith waiver. I was believing that God would bring us one because our budget was tight. I returned to my desk after lunch and I had a text from my son, Nathan, saying he had a microwave for Laura. I asked him if it was small so he sent me a picture of it. It was a small microwave that looked new. I was so excited and thanked him for it. When I got off work, I called Nathan and asked him how he found it. He said a guy he worked with gave it to him. I said, "How did that happen?" He said, "It was the strangest thing. A few of us from work went out to eat and we rode in my coworker's vehicle. One of the guys in the truck said to the driver, 'How long are you going to keep riding around in your truck with this microwave?' The man said, 'I can't seem to get rid of it. No one seems to want it, so I'm not sure what to do with it.' Nathan asked him, if he was trying to sell it and he said, "No, I am trying to give it away. It was my daughter's in college but she doesn't need it anymore." Nathan said, "I will take it off your hands. My sister is going to college and she is looking for a small microwave." He said, "It is yours then!" I told Nathan what I had prayed and how hard I had searched for one but I had prayed that God would give me one that morning. Nathan commented how neat it was that God had answered my prayer like that.

God never fails us when we trust Him. I now realize why I could not find Laura a microwave. God knew she would need one and wanted to increase my faith in Him. Weeks before I asked God for the microwave, He already had one saved for her through my son's coworker. What an awesome God we serve! Right after Nathan gave Laura the microwave, there was one advertised for sale for $35.00 on the Facebook McCurtain County Online Yard Sale. I just smiled, knowing God had saved my money and showed me that He will meet our needs when we believe Him for whatever we need. God is so amazing and He truly will meet our needs more than we can ask or think about! *"Now glory be to God, who by his mighty power at work within us is able to do far more than we would ever dare to ask or even dream of—infinitely beyond our highest prayers, desires, thoughts, or hopes."* Ephesians 3:20

Upside!

Nelda Hunkapillar

*M*y story is not that much different than thousands of others. You don't have to look far to find someone whose battles are far harder than yours. Along with these stories are also stories of hope. Hope for a cure, remission, or just more time. In the whole scheme of things, these years are just a snippet of time. We must use what time God has given us to do what we should. We can't change what is. Depend on God and His guidance through the storms.

My story began in June of 1992 when I was 43 years old. I was teaching high school vocational home economics and my husband, Terry, had his career in the forestry division. We were busy working and raising our two sons – Trent at 15 years of age and Darren at 8. I was diagnosed with non-Hodgkin's lymphoma – Stage 4. Talk about a life changer! Anyone that has ever been diagnosed or have had a family member diagnosed with cancer will tell you that once you have the word "Cancer" connected to your name – the world stands still. Denial, disbelief, fright, and many other emotions crashed into each other. These things take over your life. Your mind is frozen. What to do next? How do you tell your family? We told only close family and friends, at first

A plan was developed with my local doctor and at the MD Anderson Cancer Center in Houston. Tests started right after the 4th of July weekend. My sister and her husband, Ruby and Larry, met us there. We stayed a week getting extensive testing done. We came home to begin my long battle against cancer. The treatment protocol would be three months of Interferon injections and oral steroids. Three weeks of treatments, then one week off. Having a plan helped us to focus and start thinking forward again. My name now has a medical number forever attached to it. When you see your name on a folder bearing the Cancer Center's name, it really hits home as to what your future holds.

UPSIDE! Cancer is a word, not a sentence. I am really in this fight.

UPSIDE! *"I will lift up mine eyes unto the hills, from whence cometh my help. My help cometh from the Lord, which made heaven and earth. He will not suffer thy foot to be moved: He that keepeth thee shall not slumber. Behold, he that keepeth Israel shall neither slumber nor sleep. The Lord is thy keeper: the Lord is thy shade upon thy right hand. The sun shall not smite thee by day, nor the moon by night. The Lord shall preserve thee from all evil: he shall preserve thy soul. The Lord shall preserve thy going out and thy coming in from this time forth, and even for evermore".* Psalm 121 (KJV).

During the first two months as news spread into the community, there were daily reminders of prayers and support through cards, flowers, gifts, visits, phone calls, meals and many other uplifting moments. A few that stand out was when my neighbor Joyce brought in a meal and with tears in her eyes said, "I thought you might not feel like cooking". She gave me a much needed hug and left me in much better spirits than she found me. Another time, J. Walter Slater, one of my favorite people and neighbor who had known me all my life, brought me all the peaches his tree produced that year. Neighbors, Joann and Donna, took my son Darren to the circus one afternoon – some sense of normalcy for him. My co-workers at the high school sent me a sweatshirt and pants with their handprints on them along with a note that said I would get well since they had laid their hands on me. Everywhere signs of support. **UPSIDE!**

I felt as though I had let myself down. After all, I was the one who I could depend on to take care of me and I had failed – I had Cancer! Some people are very private about their diagnosis for various reasons. I have talked to people who were embarrassed about their cancer; some who thought they would be seen as weak and others who wanted to simply fight the big "C" on their own. I did feel that maybe I had failed but I had a great need and desire for prayers. This was bigger than me. How could people pray for my recovery if they weren't aware I was ill? I was on many church prayer lists in my community and beyond. **UPSIDE!**

During the three weeks of injections I felt like I had a really bad case of the flu. During this time it was decided I needed a hysterectomy. I was off treatments for several weeks for surgery and recovery; a time to actually feel better. **UPSIDE!**

In January, the "hard chemo" started. This consisted of three days of 24 hours per day of chemo; then a month later five days of treatment with up to 8 hours of chemo a day; then a month later a two day treatment. I went through this cycle three times. It took about 10 -11 months because treatments were sometimes delayed due to a low blood count. The treatments left me drained physically, emotionally, and mentally. Nausea, hair loss, weight loss, trips to the E.R. and fatigue so severe I could only be up a few minutes at a time. This was followed by another year of Interferon injections and steroids. There were days when I just wanted to give up. My friends and family wouldn't let me, and I knew I couldn't. The reward would be too great. **UPSIDE!**

At one point, I did not recognize my own image in a mirror. I kept thinking about my boys and how much their lives had been impacted. Many times when I had been in the bed most of the day I would watch the clock so I could be sitting up when Darren would get home from school and when Trent would get home from his after school job. My friends at school would video school performances and even some summer baseball so I would not miss out on everything. My mom and Terry's mom helped keep everything going at home. My church family brought meals three times a week for two months. I had many encouraging calls from my brother, Larry and his wife, Jean.

When an illness becomes chronic, there is a toll taken on family life and relationships. My boys saw the outpouring of love and support our family received when we were going through this tough time. All of these experiences helped shape them into the good men that they are today.

Through the chemo and interferon and, more recently, radiation treatments for breast cancer, I have learned so much about my family, my friends and myself. During this time there was a continual search for the "Upside" to keep from going under emotionally, with thoughts of wondering how treatments will affect me now and in the future; side effects and after effects. What toll will be taken on my family, jobs, marriage, etc.? What holds the cancer at bay now could cause health problems in the future. I must make the best choice I can and look for the "Upside". Sometimes you have to get worse before you get better.

My friends and family are my cheerleaders! Martha, Johnia, Donita, Kay and many others are always ready to help with whatever I need. When I'm down and can't seem to get up; discouraged and exhausted from travel and treatments- they and the Lord are always there with positive thoughts and empathy. They sign up for 'travel duty' to get me to my treatments, no questions asked; just depend on them for that day every week. They celebrate with me for good reports and end of treatments. Quality time, laughter and conversations while killing the disease inside of me. Serious talks about life, faith, God, country and family. **UPSIDE!**

It is hard to learn to accept help when you are independent and raised to stand on your own two feet. When we think we have a perfectly good plan, God has **the** perfect plan and He would have us accept any help offered. If not, we are denying others their blessing to serve and grow their servant hearts — one of God's ministries!

The lymphoma has returned twice. The treatments have not been as lengthy or harsh. I have had both hips replaced twice (AFTER EFFECTS). Summer of 2014, the breast cancer was discovered in the CT scan while having a checkup on the lymphoma. In the words of the doctor, "You don't want to hear this, but you do want to hear this". The breast cancer was taken care of with a lumpectomy and radiation. **UPSIDE!**

Through all of this, I watched my husband, who had lived with diabetes and all its side effects for years, succumb to his fight on Feb. 5, 2010. We managed through all the years, trying to maintain our new normal every day.

This journey has allowed me to look at life from a different perspective and influenced choices I made. Every day is a blessing. I have shared my experience with people I see who are struggling with their new diagnosis and those who are anxiously waiting on test results to see if treatments are working. Their body language, facial expressions and conversations are telling. I was where they are now. I am here now — today. You can be also.

God is still faithful and proves to me daily that I am here for a reason. One, I know I am a living testimony. That God is the same faithful healer yesterday, today and forever. Another reason is to give Him praise and honor as I continue to find the **UPSIDE!**

I don't remember asking "Why Me?". I just know I was in the battle of my life. By seeking treatment at a research/teaching center, maybe the doctors could learn something from my case to help others. **UPSIDE!**

My prayers were to be able to tolerate treatments then have remission; to see my sons graduate high school, then to see them graduate college. Then to see them have successful careers and strong, happy marriages. God's answer was "YES" so many times. I have seen all of that. **UPSIDE!**

A Bigger **UPSIDE!** - I have rocked three grandchildren in my arms and another one is coming in February!

Learn to handle trials, leaning on the Lord. Have a positive attitude. How you handle adversity and your attitude about the trial you are going through both determine how you will come out on the other side; bitter or better? And always look for the "Upside". You never know who will be helped by looking at your trials and how you handle them.

He Supplied My Needs

Paula Jenkins

*L*ooking back on my life I can clearly see the merciful hand of God in some crucial moments. Here are two such incidents. The first account took place one fall when my husband was going to go deer hunting. His plan was to head for deer camp, stop along the way to hunt some, then take a nap once he got to camp and then hunt until dark. He had worked the night before leaving and this is where our story begins. I received a phone call about 10 PM that day saying my husband had been in wreck and was taken to the hospital in Idabel, Ok. Evidently, he had fallen asleep behind the wheel on the way to deer camp and had an accident. The doctor said he was pretty banged up and they would keep him overnight for observation. The next day they sent him home with a neck collar. When he wanted to get up from sitting in his recliner, I would have to hold his head up and I could tell something wasn't right. I took him to the doctor's office and insisted more test be done. More x-rays showed that he had broken his neck. He was airlifted to the hospital in Texarkana, Texas. My husband claims the trip was not a pleasant one! The doctor in the ER stated it was a miracle from God that my husband wasn't dead or paralyzed as his neck was fractured in three places. One wrong move could have been tragic. He was put in traction for several days while waiting for surgery. In the end they only had to put him in a halo device. He was off work for six months.

Our second incident took place in 2010 when my husband became very ill. I took him to the ER in Idabel where the doctor thought he had a hernia and would need surgery. They sent him to McAlester, Oklahoma for the surgery. The doctor there saw him and surgery was scheduled for the next day. They ran some more tests that were needed before surgery. The doctors told us my husband was too sick to have surgery and for us to go home and see our family doctor. As we had no family doctor, I took him to the Kiamichi Medical Center where we were told my husband had cirrhosis of the liver in an advanced stage. His pancreas was not working and enzymes were entering his intestines. He was literally starving to death. All they could do was try to keep him comfortable. We stayed at my Mom's and when my husband began having symptoms we were to watch for, we took him over to Paris, Texas to the hospital. The doctor there transferred him to the O.U. Medical Center in Oklahoma City by ambulance with us following by car.

My husband's doctor at the OU Medical Center met us as we walked in and told us how serious my husband was and that his affairs needed to be in order and any other family members should be called in. Our children came and my Mom and aunt were there.

My aunt had been talking to my husband about giving his heart to the Lord and we talked to him about forgiveness and the love of God. My husband's surgery did not go well and he was put on a ventilator with drain tubes and a feeding tube. He had to be kept sedated as he kept pulling out the tubes. He was in ICU for four months. We never knew for sure if he even knew we were there. I had two jobs and had to go back to work. Our oldest daughter would go sit and read the Bible to him and so would I, when I could be there. Our youngest daughter wasn't allowed in ICU, as she was pregnant at the time. Two ministers would come and visit with him. They prayed for us all. The doctor would keep me posted on my husband's condition and called one day to let me know it was time to let him go. When my daughter arrived at the hospital, we made the decision to take him off life support. He was gone in twenty minutes

At the beginning of this ordeal, when my husband first became sick, we applied for Social Security disability. We had no insurance. We also had no place to stay. The first night there I slept in my car. After my daughter and son –in-law arrived; we stayed with his uncle's family who lived in the area. The uncle, a preacher in Dibble, Oklahoma and his wife were the sweetest and kindest people. They were such a comfort and blessing to me. I started going to Sunday morning services with them. The people were all so kind and encouraging. The church met at the Senior Citizen's Center and I started going on Thursdays to help out there. I know God put me with this couple for a reason. I can never repay them for what they did for my family and me. I know they will be rewarded in heaven.

At the hospital, I was called to the financial aid office where a Christian lady gave me a CSI form to apply for medical expenses. She also helped me get SSI benefits. I told her about my peace during this time and that I had turned my problems over to the Lord. I met with her several times and we had conversations about the Lord. She told me her husband was having a problem with un-forgiveness. I felt the Lord laid it on my heart to tell him to write a letter forgiving the offender (whom was already deceased) then destroy it and release the problem to God and let peace come to him.

After my husband died, this lady sent me a form to fill out. When I started receiving the bills from all the different hospitals they were stamped "Paid in Full".

I owe everything to God. Without His grace and mercy, I would be destitute. I could have never paid all those bills.

I hesitated to write this story. Our enemy, Satan, doesn't want people to know what God can do in desperate situations. I can truly thank Jesus for His help. I am so humbled to know He is my best friend and protector. I will never cease to thank Him for my many, many blessings.

Little Details of God's Care

Sue Kincaid

I grew up in the area north of Broken Bow, Oklahoma known as Hochatown. My family and neighbors were hard working, God fearing people who trusted God with the smallest details of their lives. Many instances in my own life revealed to me God's infinite care over His creation. Two incidents, in particular, came to mind when I was asked to write a testimony.

My uncle was plowing near my home when he became very ill. My cousins came and asked me to go get his wife. In that area there are many creeks – tributaries to the beautiful Mt. Fork River. I had to cross one to get to my aunt's house. Trying to get there as soon as possible, without thinking, I drove off into dangerously high water. There were no signs like the, "Turn around, don't drown", ones back then. I asked the Lord to help me. I made it across safely, but there were some anxious moments. When I got to my aunt's house, she asked me why I took that road. She told me that while I had been away at school a low water bridge had been built in another location that was much safer. I thank the Lord that even in my bad decision, he protected me. Also, the prayers of God's people for my uncle's recovery were answered.

The other occasion of God's care was a day when I got my car stuck. There were no hard surface roads, just dirt roads. When it rained, it was not uncommon to slide off into a ditch or simply get stuck on the road in the ruts other vehicles had made. One day I got stuck and the more I accelerated the more the wheels were spinning and digging a deeper hole with every turn. I finally gave up and started walking for help. I hadn't gone very far when I had a really strong impression to go back and try again to get the car out. I walked back, got in the car, started the engine and just drove right out of that hole. I think God performed a "Red Sea Crossing" miracle for me. It seemed like I was driving on dry ground.

It's A Miracle

Marilyn Lester

*T*he Word of God says in I John 4:18 that "*fear has torment*". Anyone who has lived in fear will agree wholeheartedly.

Even though I was raised in a Christian home, attended church regularly and received the Lord as my Savior at the age of eight, an element of fear was lurking somewhere inside me to jump out at any moment. That fear became more prevalent after becoming a mother of three boys. I was afraid a fiddleback spider would bite them as they were crawling on the floor, stick their finger in a fan with gory results, or jump in front of a car and be run over. I'd be watching and couldn't do anything to stop it. One can never be totally comfortable and at peace because of the torment of fear.

It was my practice, any time the family would be traveling more than 50 miles from home, as Don was filling the car with gas, I was inside the car writing: "In Case of Emergency" contacts, etc., etc., etc., and plastering it all over each child, in the glove box of the car, in my purse, etc. because it was not certain that we'd make it home in one piece. Fear has torment.

In my mid twenties, my husband and I began to hunger for a closer relationship with the Lord. Matthew 5:6 tells us that when you hunger and thirst, you'll be filled. Father God sent opportunities, books, witnesses, and friends— new and old that began bringing deeper revelation of our wonderful God and His Word. We learned in I John 4:4 that we are "overcomers" because of the "greater one" living is us. I John 4:5 confirms the fact because we are "believers". Then, I John 5:14-15 tells us that we can have "confidence" in Him because He will do what He has said, if we ask according to His Will, believing.

The Word of God became my best friend. My determined purpose was to know Him—*"progressively become more deeply and intimately acquainted with Him. . . and come to know the power outflowing from Him."* (excerpt taken from Philippians 3:10 Amplified Bible)

Every day was spent reading, meditating, and saying out loud the verses from Isaiah 26:3; Isaiah 54:17; Luke 10:19; and the whole 91st chapter of Psalm—especially verses 11 and 12 where it says God gives His angels charge over us for protection. The angels will pick us up, even when we just stump our toe.

I John 4:18 not only says that *"fear has torment"*, but that *"perfect love casts out fear"*. As I spent time with God in His Word, I became acquainted with my Father Who IS LOVE. That understanding helped me to believe that He will do what He has said He will do. Read Numbers 23:19.

Now, instead of making notes for "In Case of Emergency", I spent time reading Psalm 91. In fact, on the trip that included the miracle, I read Psalm 91 in three different versions of the Bible. It was done, not because of fear, but to feed my faith.

The Scene: My folk's house in Oklahoma City. They had an above ground pool in the backyard. It was 4 feet deep. Because the yard was quite slanted, the back of the pool was above ground, while the front (or house side) of the pool was only a foot above ground. There was not a ladder and the sides were a bit slick because the chemicals were not balanced just right.

My dad, a wonderful man who never sat very long in one place, had the boys invite the neighbor boys to come swim. He sat patiently beside the pool watching them. Our youngest son, Ross, had a child's blowup ring under his arms and around his chest. (Can I be a little facetious in saying that the first miracle was my dad sitting there for an hour and a half?) But, when he was ready for the boys to get out, he gave them the "everyone out" holler, pulled the blown up ring off Ross and proceeded to shuffle all the boys out the gate. Dad and our other two sons went out to the front lawn and began raking leaves.

After several minutes, Ross was crying in terror at the back door. I went to the door, grabbed a beach towel, wrapped him up and began to console him. Immediately, I asked, "What's the matter?" Through tears and sobbing he said,

"I falled in the pool and couldn't get out?" My first reaction was to look all around the back yard to see who had helped him out of the pool. There was no one there. I said, "How did you get out?" He said, "I don't know." I said, "Did you swim out?" (We'd been trying to teach him how to take a couple of strokes, but he had not mastered that, yet.) He said, "No."

I sat down in the chair and began to rock and console him. As I sat there, the Lord whispered softly, "It was Me." I started thanking and praising Him. After all, how many 3-year-old children fall into a swimming pool with no one around and come tell you about it? My heart was flooded with thanksgiving and praise.

Continuing in praise and thanksgiving to my Heavenly Father, I had a mini vision. I saw Ross at the bottom of the pool. He was facing toward the house. Then I saw 4 large angels in white robes (no wings), each placing both of their hands on his little bottom, lifting him out of the pool. Ross threw his leg over the side and ran up to the house. It was just as Psalm 91:11 & 12 said, *"For he shall give his angels charge over thee, to keep thee in all thy ways. They shall bear thee up in their hands. . ."*

Yes, indeed. Fear does have torment. But, GOOD NEWS, perfect love casts out fear. God IS Love. *". . . Has He said, and will He not do it."* Glory to God!

The Ice Dispenser

Marilyn Lester

My parents bought a new refrigerator with an ice and water dispenser in the door. That was a novelty to our children who had never seen such a fun way to get a drink.

While our oldest son, Steve, was at Little League baseball practice about 20 miles from where we lived, the other two boys and I went to my folks' house. It was only 3 or 4 miles from the ball diamond.

While there, barefooted Ross (22 months old) picked up a drinking glass and started toward the refrigerator. His body was in forward motion; but his bare feet acted like a suction to the floor, keeping his feet in the same place. That caused him to begin to fall. As he fell, he dropped the glass, causing it to break leaving a sharp, jagged, broken glass upright on the floor. He reached out his hands to catch himself. When he did, his little chubby hand landed on the broken glass causing about a 5/8-inch deep gash in his hand. How could a baby's hand be that thick, was my thought. The deep, U-shaped laceration extended from the wrist up across his palm and around to the base of the thumb on his right hand. I was sitting in a chair within arm's reach of Ross. All I had to do was lean over, turn him over and pick him up. That close, and I could not stop the accident.

My parents were on their way home from sponsoring a high school senior trip. Our two youngest boys and I were at the house alone. It was 15 miles to the nearest hospital--2 miles to our little western Oklahoma town. Ross was bleeding profusely. Should I go toward the hospital, or should I drive the 2 miles to town? The service station at the edge of town was where we traded. Certainly, someone would be there that could drive us. But, if not, Grif—the owner of the station and a friend—would surely help me. That's what folks in small towns do! A neighbor "just happened" to be there and quickly jumped in the driver's seat as I jumped out, carrying Ross, and running around the car to the passenger's seat. Praise the Lord for good neighbors and friends! God had him there right when he was needed.

Our family doctor came to the hospital to assess the situation. Ross' condition was far too severe for anything to be done by the family doctors at the small community hospital. Even though it took a couple of hours, the doctor found a specialist in Oklahoma City that could do the needed surgery. That was another 2½ hours drive.

Someone had picked up Steve from baseball practice. Others had gotten Don, my husband, off the tractor and out of the field—it was before the days of cell phones—and to the hospital where we were. A friend had picked up extra clothes for me. Since I had been mowing I was dirty with green grass stain, etc. My parents had come home to a bloody, broken glass mess, not having any idea what had gone on there. Finding out what had happened, they came to the hospital to get Brent, our other son, who was with me. While we were at the hospital waiting for the doctor to make the decisions, our friend who had driven us, took our car and cleaned out all the blood, etc. The car was clean and ready for us to make the trip to OKC. Again, praise the Lord for good neighbors and friends!

Don, Ross and I started the 2½ hours trip to OKC. Our family doctor had given Ross something to ease him on the trip. As I prayed, knowing we also had many friends praying, the scripture continually rang over and over in my spirit *"The effectual fervent prayer of a righteous man availeth much."* (James 4:16b.)

A group of nurses greeted us when we arrived at Presbyterian Hospital. After calling the doctor to come, they began to prep Ross for surgery. We asked about how long the surgery would be. "Oh, surgery usually lasts between 1½ to 2 hours," they said.

Ross' room was adjacent to the nurse's desk for their ease in caring for him after surgery. One army cot was placed in the room for Don and me to sleep on. After taking Ross out of the room, we knelt on the floor beside the cot and began to pray. *"The effectual fervent prayer of a righteous man availeth much."* (James 4:16b.) We knew that our Father God hears and answers prayers. *"My help comes from the LORD, Who made heaven and earth."* (Psalm 121:2) We have a Divine invitation in Hebrews 4:16 to "come boldly" to God's throne *"that we may obtain mercy and find grace to help in time of need"*. We needed God to guide the hands of the surgeon as he performed his skill in the operating room.

One hour passed. Two hours passed. Approximately 2½ hours later, the doctor came to our room and explained that Ross had severed every working mechanism in his little hand. The surgery was only half complete. He then returned to the OR. We continued to pray.

Four and a half hours after the surgery started, it was finished. The doctor came to explain that everything the doctor had to work with in Ross' hand was smaller than a thread. He would certainly have to have at least one more surgery. It would be more extensive than the one just performed. Probably even more than one additional surgery would be necessary for the hand to be useable.

Having any feeling in that hand was not a given, either. However, being only 22 months old, there was a possibility that the nerves would grow back. The doctor explained that if they didn't grow back and he never regained any feeling in that hand, it would be better that the hand be amputated because Ross could lay it in a fire and never know it.

A couple of days later, the three of us left the hospital. Ross had a cast that went from the tips of his fingers to the top of his arm. It was bent at the elbow with his hand and fingers curved toward his wrist. It made a great weapon to use on a brother's head if they bugged him. (Not too proud of that part!)

Three weeks later, the cast was cut off. The saw that the doctor used scared Ross and he tried to pull away from it. As the cast came off, Ross' little finger and thumb moved slightly. We were ecstatic. There was movement! PTL! We showed everyone we saw how he could move the little finger and thumb.

Before we left the doctor's office he said, "Don't baby this child. Make him do things for himself." "But couldn't the stiches come loose?" I asked. "Yes. Everything I did could come undone. But, if you don't make him use the hand, he will completely lose the use of it," the doctor admonished.

So began the therapy. About 6 weeks later, we had to start straightening each finger, 10 times each, 3 times a day. Later, bending each finger backward. Finally, painfully bending each finger even farther. Ross learned to count to ten as we did the therapy each day. He would sobbingly say, "wa-wa-wa-one; ta-ta-ta-two; fa-fa-fa-free. ." and so on.

"You may hear a loud pop and feel something give way," the doctor instructed. "That's good. It has to happen. That's the scar tissue breaking loose. That has to happen or his fingers will be permanently curved, stiff and useless." Every time we did therapy, I dreaded hearing and feeling that snap. IT NEVER HAPPENED. The scar tissue didn't develop. PTL, again.

At the 6-month check-up with the surgeon, he asked us to make another appointment one year from the surgery. The only reason for that appointment was for him to see the amazing results of such a devastating accident.

Not long after the surgery, radio commentator, Paul Harvey, mentioned on his broadcast that hand surgery is more intricate and complicated than open-heart surgery. *"Behold, I am the LORD, the God of all flesh. Is there anything too hard for Me?"* (Jeremiah 32:27.) That hand has not been, nor is now, limited although the feeling is somewhat different than the other hand. Oh, yes, he's left-handed; but he was trying to be that before the accident.

Rejoice by Choice

Viola McEuin

"Always be full of joy in the Lord, I say it again — Rejoice."

Philippians 4:4

"Rejoice always. Pray without ceasing, give thanks in all circumstances, for this is the will of God concerning you."

1 Thessalonians 5:16-18

God wants us to rejoice and we have every reason to do so. We are not told to be long faced, irritable, negative, complaining people. Jesus said not to rejoice about the spirits being subject to them but to rejoice that their names were written in heaven. (Luke 10:20) If we have, by faith, accepted the salvation Jesus offers, we should be rejoicing. Think of the benefits He brings to us: His abiding presence while here on earth and an eternal home in heaven. He provides for our earthly needs. If I need healing in my body, His Word declares, *"By His stripes we were healed"*. I have had sick times including several surgeries and God has been with me through it all.

One time in particular, He provided some very tangible physical, spiritual, financial and emotional things for my family and me. He did all these in one short span of time. I had a double hernia surgery and was going to the doctor in Paris, Texas to have the staples taken out. We had a 2003 Pontiac van that occasionally would not start. I had a new 'lifetime warranty' starter put on just one year prior to this incident. When we were ready to leave the doctor's office, the van would not start. I could sometimes fiddle with it and it would finally start, but not this day. I had been praying for God to show me how to get it fixed. I tried for 30 minutes or longer and could not get it to start. It was afternoon and we were tired, hungry, and in need of a restroom. We finally went back into the doctor's office and used the restroom, then went across the street to a meat market. The market had everything one needed for a meal. We made our purchases and went back to the van. Again, I tried to start the van to no avail. I prayed, "Lord, we need help". We were one and a half hours away from home. The Lord assured me that all my prayers of needing the van to finally be fixed would be answered. We called for a tow truck from the phone in the doctor's office and asked to be taken to the nearest repair shop. When the truck pulled up, it was quite an ordeal for us to climb into that huge 'monster' tow truck. Once we arrived at the repair shop, it was a climb to get down from it. By the grace of God, neither of us was hurt.

After about 15 minutes in the waiting room, the manager of the shop came and said the van started right up. I was flabbergasted! He asked several questions and said he thought it was the starter. He went out and came back with the report. It was a bad starter. So much for that lifetime warranty. It was sure a short lifetime. The manager told me he would have to charge me for a new starter but would have it fixed in no time. His fee was just over $450.00. There were times when we would not have had the funds to handle that fee, but I was overjoyed to pay him. Right before I had my surgery a neighbor had given me $250 to help out during the time I would be off. Then a friend came by and gave me $200. I was also able to get my money back on that "lifetime warranty" starter. What a faithful God we serve. In that one day, He provided so many things in so many ways; cooler weather, a place for lunch, strength to climb into the cab of the tow truck, a shop manager that was kind and knowledgeable, and funds to pay for what was needed. There are so many reasons to rejoice so, "Rejoice by Choice".

You might ask how I learned that lesson, so here is that story: In 2003, I went to work at Wal-Mart in Broken Bow, Oklahoma after my husband passed away. In prayer, I felt the Lord was telling me, "In that position you will have insurance and benefits". One day the manager called several of us in to tell us that we would have to transfer to the new Super Center in Idabel if we wanted to keep our jobs. I didn't have a vehicle to drive back and forth but I felt the Lord telling me 'do whatever you need to do to protect your job'. So I put my car in the shop and drove a loaner car until mine was repaired. I was now working in Idabel at the old Wal-Mart getting it ready to close, so the new Super Center could open. After 2-3 weeks of working in this position, I thought I would go nuts. It was like a giant garage sale of marked down items. People were fighting in the aisles, stealing things from others shoppers and being disrespectful. I cried a lot those first weeks; I just didn't want to be there. One day while on my break, the Lord convicted me for my attitude. "Quit acting like a spoiled child, quit whining and start shining! Rejoice by Choice". I told the Lord, "OK Lord, but you will have to help me, for I don't want to". "I know and I will help you", He said and He did! From that time on I began to smile and be a friendly cashier. (But I did listen for a chance to go back to Broken Bow.) Soon the Idabel store was open and I put in a transfer and went back to the Broken Bow store after only three months. Thanks be to God!!

I learned a lot in those three months. I still don't understand the company's logic on how all the moving and hiring, etc. took place but I do, however, understand more about my faithful God. I know He loves me. He wants me to do the best I can at whatever He gives me to do. He wants me to "Shine – not whine". He wants me to "Rejoice by Choice". I also know that He will help me do exactly that, come what may. He in me is the overcomer.

John 16:33 states, *"These things I have spoken unto you, that in me ye might have peace. In the world ye shall have tribulation but be of good cheer. I have overcome the world."*

Mother's Prayer

Frank Meddock

I was 10 years old, about 85 pounds and in the fifth grade. It was early spring and a beautiful, crisp, cool day. I was standing on the bank of the Mountain Fork River, in the Beavers Bend State Park near Broken Bow, Oklahoma.

My mother was what I now call a "Prayer Warrior". She would pray out loud for extended periods of time and it seemed she covered all the bases. But my mother was miles from where her ten-year-old son was considering doing something really dumb.

I was participating in the Boy Scouts Spring Camp in the Park. There were fifty or sixty boys and several adults at the campsite, but I wasn't at the campsite, but up the river at the traditional boathouse and swimming area. The facilities were closed during the off-season months and while the river was up.

We, about a dozen boys, were at the riverfront. There were no adults present. Some of the older boys began to challenge each other to swim the river. I didn't participate in the challenge, but as a couple of the older boys lined up to take the challenge, I pondered the idea that I could do it. As they jumped into the water, I jumped in behind them. I gained on them and passed them showing off my stuff, and then looking back, I saw that both of them had turned back. The water was cold and the current swift. I had spent a lot of time on the same river where we lived near it, a few miles north at what is now known as the Old Hochatown. I wasn't afraid of the river. I knew I could do it.

I had to swim aggressively into the current to avoid being washed down stream, but was still confident of a successful crossing. Then while still in the swift current, it was like someone shot me with a 12-gage shotgun. The muscles in my stomach locked up tight, drawing my head toward my knees. My legs were disabled and my head was under water. I paddled furiously with my hands as dog paddles with his front legs. I eventually got my head above water and gasped for breath. I was breathing but not crossing the river. I don't remember anything else while in the river current.

The next thing I remember was seeing the gravel on the bottom of the river, as it appeared to be moving back and forth toward my face. I was floating face down with my eyes open in two or three feet of clear water. The sun was shining against the clean gravel on the bottom that glistened toward me. I was behind a big flat rock that extruded out into the river and was giving me shelter from the river current. I pulled myself to the bank with my hands.

I was still drawn up like a roly-poly, dysfunctional except for my hands and arms. I drug myself onto the bank like an alligator with no back legs. I don't remember any pain as I was dragging myself out of the water or for a little while after. I laid in the sun, barely out of the water. Then the pain came back. There was a knot the size of a softball and as hard as a baseball extruding from the middle of my stomach. The pain was excruciating. My friends across the river must have heard me groaning as I beat the knot with both fists, groaning louder with each lick until it released, and it did release.

Within minutes after the muscles relaxed the pain subsided, I stood up and looked across the river. No one appeared to be getting a boat or to do anything else to help. That is when I realized I was going to have to swim back across the river. This time, with a little more thought, I walked up the river bank, along the mountain base about 100 yards, and swam with the current going down stream, instead of against it, as it was with the first crossing. The current took me comfortably to the landing where my loyal friends were waiting. Some mocked and made fun of me, while others complimented me.

As I later pondered the event, I came to the conclusion that my mother must have been praying and that it was my mother's prayer that took me from the deep swift water to the sheltered place, behind the rock.

I don't ever want to come up short in praying for those I love, that they will also find a sheltered place when needed and, most of all, that they will find the sheltered place behind the (living) rock, Jesus Christ.

My Story

Brett Miller

I grew up in a respectable family. I was taught good moral behavior and knew right from wrong. My mother made sure my brother and I attended church with her every Sunday. My brother made a decision for Christ at an early age and as usual, I was compelled to follow him at whatever he did, so I was also baptized. Admittedly, there was little change in my life after the event. I was an honor roll student and found my identity mostly in baseball because I knew I was good at it. I was smaller than my classmates and I didn't regard myself as particularly handsome. The effort I poured into the baseball field helped our team to achieve two state championships.

Then I graduated and didn't really know what to do with myself. I was very lonely and I picked up the phone and called a cousin of mine to come and visit. In high school, he influenced me towards drinking a lot of beer. He was very popular and I liked to be associated with him. I thought others would think I was "cool", if I drank with him. He showed up at college and I was shocked when he pulled out a bag of methamphetamine; I had never seen any. I told him he shouldn't be doing that stuff. He tried to get me to use some of it. The first several times I refused and then one day I gave in. I tried it and it was like a rush of adrenaline coursed through my body, my heart raced, I felt euphoria overtake me, and it was like all my cares were gone.

For two years, I was a slave to meth. I lost so much weight that I looked like a bag of bones. My memory started failing; sometimes I wouldn't sleep for 4 or 5 days in a row. I could think of nothing else other than getting high and my body craved the drug. I started raiding patches of marijuana I found in the woods and I would steal enough of it to pay for my habits. I thought of ending my own life quite a lot. One day at the parking lot of the campus bookstore, I ran into the girl I always thought was so beautiful from high school. I never thought she would give me a second look, but that day she gave me her phone number. I spent most nights at her apartment pretending like I was just hanging out. It finally became apparent I was pursuing her and much to my surprise, she didn't mind the idea. We became quite serious. She put up with my ways of drugging and drinking for some time and finally somehow she talked me into attending church with her on Sunday. I knew my life had never really been changed and honestly I came to grips with the fact that I was lost, having never known the transforming power of Jesus. I walked the isle, I was baptized, but the drugs and alcohol didn't give up easy. I found myself high with a nosebleed on my apartment floor one day and felt very much alone. I cried out to God that day and told Him I was not able to let go of the poison that was killing me, but if He would help me I would sure be glad to let Him do it.

From that day forward, I began to win the war. There were still hard fought battles and some setbacks, but the tide began to prevail in my favor. For 15 years, I have been sober, drug free, the faithful husband of the love of my life, and the father of two Godly children, ages 8 and 10. For 13 years, I have been preaching the Gospel. I can't imagine what my story would be like if the Lord had not allowed me to hit "rock bottom" in order to open my eyes to my greatest inward need.

The Divine Appointment

Kelly Mills

Having grown up a preacher's kid (PK), I attended church every time the doors were open and we were always there at least thirty minutes early. We were taught, to be respectful of the church house, our elders, and our parents. We learned the value of serving others, made many dear friends, both young and old. I look back with fondness on my adventures as a PK. As you can imagine, I heard many "hellfire and brimstone" sermons, jumped at many a slammed fist, and witnessed many altar calls filled with weeping, broken-hearted parishioners. I also made many of those trips to the altar, three to be exact, during my childhood. Each time I was equally as terrified of hell and was certain that I did not want my afterlife to consist of a blazing inferno filled with weeping and gnashing of teeth, where the worm never dies. I never remember simply following other kids down, I was genuinely terrified of hell and would do whatever I needed to do to avoid that awful fate. So, after each time at the altar I was systematically dunked as well. Now I know, I was just getting wet.

For many years I walked this earth, feeling fairly secure with my place in heaven. I sauntered through life with no real conviction to help those who were lost and no passion for Christ. Sure, I went to church every Sunday and Wednesday night, attended small group, participated in Bible studies, and even sang in the choir. Then, when I was twenty-three, and pregnant with my youngest son, I attended a revival at my local church. That night, March 8,1997, the minute I walked in the doors I knew this would be no ordinary revival. I didn't know it then, but now I know that the Holy Spirit was present and he was waiting on me to show up. He began to work on my heart to the point where I couldn't even sing. The music was dynamic and unfamiliar to me, which made it exciting and new. I don't even remember if my husband was around. I heard or saw nothing but what God intended that night. When the evangelist spoke, the words were resonating in my spirit. It was like he was talking to me. I knew, without a shadow of a doubt why I was there that night. It was a divine appointment like no other. The evangelist began to count down and tell the audience that if they felt the wooing of the Spirit to come, "don't wait", "jump up", "right where you are standing", "don't walk, run down the aisle". I knew I had to move, but being 8 months pregnant; there was no running for me. I waddled, as quickly as possible, to the front and fell on my knees. A mighty man of God, who knew my family, was waiting to talk with me. He poured his heart out to me and allowed me to do the same to Jesus.

For the FIRST time in my life, my acceptance of Christ was not situational or based on fear. It was a complete and utter surrender to the will of God in my life. I simply accepted Christ as my Savior and allowed the Holy Spirit to enter into the tabernacle of my body. It was a day that I will never forget, it was a calling that I can never deny, and it is a future that I cannot botch no matter how much I fail. My faith and my hope is secure in Christ and my goal now is not to stay out of hell (although that IS important) but to take as many people to heaven with me, as possible. I thank God every day for men and women, who are willing to be obedient to the call to pastor a church, evangelize a city, plant a church or go to a foreign land for Him. Their obedience is the reason I can write this testimony today. I can only hope that in this time I have on earth, I will be obedient and impact the lives of many with whom I come in contact with for Christ.

My Long Journey Home

Shelia Sparkman

*I*n January 2002, I was in Austin, Texas at an administrators meeting. I planned to stay Thursday and Friday night and come back home on Saturday. When I woke on Friday morning, a freak ice storm had hit Central Texas. Weather forecast called for more bad weather. I decided to start home early and thus avoid any problems, or so I thought. It is approximately 385 miles from Austin to Texarkana.

I called the highway patrol headquarters about the road conditions and was told the roads were okay; so I headed out. I made it from Austin to Greenville, Texas in my usual time. I stopped in Greenville at my Uncle Jerry's pawnshop for a break and to check on the roads ahead of me. It seemed the vehicles I had been meeting had a lot of ice on them. I called again to check the condition of the interstate from Greenville to Texarkana, which was where I was headed. I got an "All Clear" message for no interstate closings. After a short rest, I hit the road again. I made it to Sulphur Springs but the roads were not in the best of conditions. That was only about 30 miles from my Uncle's pawnshop. I was again reassured the interstate was still open. It was getting late in the afternoon and I was starting to see semi-trucks along the side of the road.

Being by myself and desperately wanting to get home and off the road, I drove onward. About 4:00 PM, I was approaching Mt. Pleasant, Texas and was about 60 miles from home! The first exit for Mt. Pleasant was where the highway patrol detoured all traffic off the interstate due to the icy conditions and the wrecks that had already happened. No one told anyone anything. They just waved us on to the detour. I thought to myself that the traffic would only be detoured around Mt. Pleasant and back onto the interstate for the short 60 miles I needed to go. Unfortunately, the traffic that was bumper to bumper was directed onto a two-lane highway that went towards Texarkana. I was now traveling on a two-lane highway on two inches of sleet and ice in bumper-to-bumper traffic – and at a snails' pace! I said a short but desperate prayer, "Lord, I'm in a bad spot here. I'm in a strange car, on an icy highway, with nothing to eat or drink but a bottle of water and a package of peanut butter crackers, traveling in heavy traffic and at about 5 mph. I need your help, Lord. I have never driven on ice like this before and I am scared. Give me peace and calm and the knowledge I need to get me through this. Thank you Father, Amen".

I saw lots of cars that had slid off the road. Several drivers became impatient and tried to pass. Nine times out of ten, I would see those same drivers in the ditch further on. I knew the Lord was with me. Have you ever traveled ten hours without making a restroom stop? I did. I never once got hungry or had the urge to make a rest stop. I stayed on the phone a lot talking to my husband. When I wasn't talking to him, I was talking to the Lord. I finally made it home around 2:00 am. A drive that should have taken an hour, took ten hours. It was one of the worse nights of my life. I know who was watching over me, my Father in Heaven.

Jesus was with me that night, of that I am sure. He gave me His peace and guided my hands as I drove that treacherous road. This was an experience I will never forget and I know now that, *"I can do all things through Christ which strengtheneth me"*. Philippians 4:13 *"Casting all your care upon him: for he careth for you"*. 1 Peter 5:7 Praise the Lord!

Marriage Healing Testimony

Shelly Stevenson

May 26th, 2004 began as just an ordinary day. I woke up and got ready for work as usual. It was beautiful and sunny. (My husband, Jamie, hadn't been himself, but he assured me it was work stress.) I left for work and when I opened my car door there was a white envelope in the seat with my name on it. In the time it took to read a letter, my whole world would change and this ordinary day would be the beginning of an extraordinary unfolding of miraculous events that God would perform to save my family.

My husband, Jamie, wanted a divorce. He was in love with someone else. We were two weeks away from our seventeenth wedding anniversary. We had a beautiful 15 ½ year old daughter. He had just given me one of the sweetest Mother's Day cards and I was in total shock. I truly felt like Satan was trying to make a mockery of my faith and everything I had ever believed in, but immediately God planted a seed of faith in my heart to trust Him to save our marriage.

My devotion reading that day was Isaiah 41:10 *"Do not be afraid, for I am with you. Do not be dismayed, for I am your God. I will strengthen you and help you. I will uphold you with my victorious right hand."* God gave me another scripture, *"Can these dry bones live?"* and another *"Surely the arm of the Lord is not too short to save nor His ear to dull to hear."* Then he reminded me, *"Is anything too difficult for the Lord?"* People called to share scriptures. I got books both through the mail and hand delivered to me. I would go into church services where I didn't know the pastor or speaker and get a Word from God. I even received a Word from God from my Pastor at the Redland United Methodist Church, Gene VanAlstyne, at a Wednesday night Bible study. One word I received from a man I didn't know was, "God has seen everything the enemy has brought against your family and He is going to restore everything the enemy has stolen." Every time I felt faint in my faith, God would send encouragement.

While everyone wanted to blame Jamie, God began showing me areas of weakness in my own life. As a matter of fact, the Lord spoke to my heart and said, "I don't want to hear anything about what Jamie has done or is doing, Shelly. This is between me and you." I had a lot to learn about being a Godly wife, learning about submission. I had a lot of unforgiveness toward Jamie for things that had happened early in our marriage, even before marriage. I had built up walls in order to protect myself. Jamie had never had my whole heart because the truth was I was afraid to trust him with it. As God began to reveal these things to me, I repented and made Him a promise, "Lord I will do anything you tell me to do." I meant it. I learned a powerful prayer, "Lord, change me."

Jamie really wanted this divorce, but for some reason was unwilling to file. I swore that I wouldn't, but in the end gave in to the pressure. The day in February, 2005 that I filed, I told God, "God, I just filed for divorce but you are bigger than these papers and if you don't want this to happen, you can stop it." It ran in the McCurtain Gazette for everyone to see. In the natural, it really did seem pretty hopeless. Every time I would get a word from God, the situation would get worse. Satan was trying with all of his might to get me to stop believing and some days were really hard.

About six months later, out of the blue, Jamie called one day and asked me if our divorce was final. The truth was I didn't know. It was paid for, filed and we had both signed the papers but I had never received any notification on going to court or the status of it. He said, "If it's not final can you have them stop it?" I called Kenneth Farley's office and asked. His secretary said she would check on it and when she came back to the phone she asked if Ken could give me a call back. I could tell something was wrong so I just asked her what it was. She told me she didn't know how it had happened but after we signed the papers they were misfiled and were never sent over to the judge. I knew how it had happened, God had intervened and the divorce was officially stopped. Jamie didn't move back home that day, but God was working. I continued to faithfully pray for my family.

In the meantime, God did numerous miracles on behalf of our family. One day In April 2006, I got a call from an old high school friend, Dr. Twana Farley Smith. She was a dentist in Antlers and she asked if I would go to work for her. I really wasn't interested. Moving to Antlers, Oklahoma was not in my plans. Two weeks later, she called again saying she was serious and needed some help in the office. The Holy Spirit prompted me to begin to pray about it. I shared this with Jamie and of all things, he said he thought he would like to come home and make the move with me. He put some applications in with a few businesses in the Antlers area.

One day, I was at my desk at the OSU extension office in Idabel and just suddenly felt completely overwhelmed. The past year and a half had been so stressful, working full time, going to school at night, trying to be a good mother, trying to not lose faith in the miracle God had promised me, all the while under constant attack from the enemy. No one thought me letting Jamie come home was a good idea. No one, but God. I wasn't even sure that I was sure, so I went to the bathroom, got down on my knees and prayed that if it was truly His will that I move to Antlers and for Jamie to come with me that he would get a better job than he currently had and a company car. I got up, went back to my office and the minute I sat down the phone rang. It was Miller Office Equipment in Antlers. The lady, Sharon Kinder, said, "Your husband came in a couple of weeks ago and applied for a job and I have never lost all of someone's paperwork before, but I have lost his and got your number from Dr. Smith. We want to offer him a job." It turned out to be a higher paying job and he would get a company car. God also miraculously provided a rent house, too.

Our daughter graduated from High School in May 2006 and we immediately packed up and moved to Antlers, Ok. I was still going to church alone. On March 30th, 2007 my mother, Sandy Bozarth, went home to be with the Lord. Jamie was asked to be a pallbearer. The following Sunday was Easter Sunday. Our daughter asked Jamie if he would go to church with us and HE DID. He was hit or miss, at first, but eventually came every Sunday. God was really working on him.

In the fall of 2007, Jamie walked the aisle of the Moyers Baptist Church and gave his heart to Jesus. He was baptized October 7th, 2007 and his life has never been the same. Since that day, we have worked for a year and a half as youth leaders with the teens at the church and drove the van. We now teach an adult Sunday school class and host home Bible study once a month. We are active in the nursing home ministry and helped out in the nursery and with children's church. Next year on June 12th, 2017 we will celebrate our 30th wedding anniversary.

After our daughter's first visit home to Antlers from college in the fall of 2006, she sent us the sweetest note. It read, "It was so nice to come home to my whole family again." God has truly done abundantly more than I could have ever thought or imagined to ask. Some days I can't even believe this is really my life, but it is and God deserves ALL the glory. We are a living testament to the truth that NOTHING is impossible with God!

Jesus, My Deliverer

Carol Swift

I had smoked for 40 years. I started when I was 15 years old. Through the years, I tried many times to quit. I tried cold turkey many times and failed. I tried the patches, the pills and the gum. They all failed. The thing that bothered me most was that I knew I could never be for the Lord all he wanted me to be, as long as I smoked.

On November 19, 1992 I told God, "I'm sorry I'm so weak Lord but I can't quit smoking and I'm so very tired of trying. I'll not smoke in front of my grandchildren and I'll never smoke in my house again, but I'm just not strong enough to quit". About an hour later as I was in my car going to town, I reached for a cigarette. It was like a huge barrel was above me. God's audible voice said, "That's the only hold Satan has on you". I laid the cigarette down but after a moment I decided I only imagined that voice and reached again for the cigarette. This time God said, "This is of Satan". I knew without a doubt it was the Lord and that I did not imagine it. I threw all my cigarettes, my lighters and a rock ashtray I kept in the car out the car window. When I got home, I threw all the cigarettes I had there away.

To this day, I have never craved a cigarette. God totally delivered me from smoking. I didn't tell a soul, not even my husband, for a week. I was so in awe of what God had done for me. It was so wonderful to wake up in the morning and not have that craving for a cigarette. *What a Miracle! What a Blessing! Thank you God!!*

I begged and pleaded with God to deliver me from smoking literally hundreds of times. I would think on and stand on the scripture in the book of Mark

11: 22-24. *"Jesus said unto them, Have faith in God. For verily I say unto you, That whosoever shall say unto this mountain, be thou removed, and be cast into the sea; and shall not doubt in his heart, but shall believe that those things which he saith shall come to pass, he shall have whatsoever he saith. Therefore I say unto you what things so ever ye desire, when ye pray, believe that ye receive them and ye shall have them".*

My deliverance didn't come. He taught me that my heart had to be in the right place to get my prayers answered. I gave up on myself, and then He took over. I got out of the way and turned it over to Him.

Thank you God for your patience and love. *"Delight thyself also in the Lord; and he shall give thee the desires of thine heart".* Psalm 37:4.

Our Son

Denise Webb

Our son, Kasen, was born on December 27, 2000, 5 weeks premature but otherwise healthy. At the end of January or first part of February, we decided to drive to Paris to eat dinner with family. It was a very cold night. On the way home, down a rural farm to market road, our 1993 Chevrolet truck began making a horrible knocking noise. The oil pressure dropped to nothing and the heater started blowing cold air. This was before we had cell phones. We were on a dark road, with a premature baby, our 7 year-old daughter and a 12 year old cousin and a truck that sounded like it was going to blow up any minute. I was terrified. I looked at my husband and asked, "What are we gonna do?" He replied, "Stopping won't help because we can't stay on the side of the road with the kids in the cold. Start praying and we are going to drive as far as we can make it."

I bundled the kids up in a blanket and we both started praying hard. I was so scared that we were going to be stranded with our tiny baby and the other kids on the side of the road. Everyone was very quiet. The only noise was the knocking motor and my whispered prayers. Suddenly the knocking stopped. The oil pressure came back to normal. The heat got warm again. The truck started running perfectly and we made it the rest of the way home, without incident.

The next day, my husband was checking over the truck and could find no reason for what happened. We drove that truck for another 3 or 4 years daily without any incident. We still own the truck and in a few months, when Kasen turns 16, that will be the truck he will drive. We have no doubt that God healed our truck and kept our babies safe that cold night almost 16 years ago.

God's Provision

Millie Westerman

My church was in the beginning phase of a capital campaign to raise funds for our new church building. The leaders of the church got together to pray and ask for God's continued blessing and guidance as we began the project. While we were praying God gave me a vision. The vision was of a man with black shiny shoes who was writing a check for $20,000. God told me that this man did not go to our church and he wasn't even a believer in Jesus Christ but he had seen how God was using our church and the good we do for our community.

At first I didn't really want to share this vision as I never know if the visions I see will come to fruition or not. After a little while and a lot of stirring by the Holy Spirit I did share what I saw with the other leaders. Several weeks went by, we completed our Capital Campaign and we met our goal. But we hadn't received a check. I began to feel a little self-conscious, and after a couple more weeks kind of forgot.

One Sunday after church, I was checking the church office mail and there was a small hand written envelope. These are always exciting because they are usually a thank you or testimony! I opened the envelope and there IT was. A check. Nothing more, no note, no letter. A check for $20,000. The man who wrote the check did not go to our church. After checking with our lead overseer I found out he is a man connected with Digi-Key Corp. He lives hundreds of miles away and does not believe in Jesus. I was told that he has seen the things our church does for the community and wanted to contribute! Praise God for His provision and His working in each of our lives

The Blessings of the Lord

Millie Westerman

My husband and I have five children and work hard to stay on budget in order to provide for our family. One day, finances were extra tight but we needed groceries. I went to the store and carefully calculated as I selected my groceries. There was a wonderful sale on meat and I got several different kinds that would last our family for a few weeks. When I got up to the checkout my calculations appeared to be off. I sat and stared as the total on the screen rose and rose. My heart sank as my limit was reached before ANY of the meat was rung up. I started to complain in my heart, angry that I couldn't get my meat. I sulkily walked back, embarrassed as I put back all of the meat. I went home and put away the groceries I was able to get and went about my day.

The next day, I received a call from a couple from church that was moving. My friend Karli said, "Millie, we have a deep freeze full of meat, and we can't take it with us. We thought of you and were wondering if you could use some meat?" I couldn't believe it. When I went to Karli's house she told me that her father was a beef cattle farmer and he kept her deep freeze stocked. She opened the freezer and gave me some large garbage bags. I packed up the meat and left her house with three large bags stuffed full of quality meat. I went home with meat "overflowing". We were blessed with so much that after stuffing our freezer full we had leftover. We were able to bless two other families with free meat! God heard my selfish and childish complaining and blessed me in spite of myself.

Strength in Times of Need

Melissa (Clay) Wilson

December 9, 2010

As a normal mom of teenagers, I was pretty much dreading going all the way into town just to drop my son, Hunter, and his girlfriend off at a basketball tournament. But as that "mother's guilt" started working on me and my son saying, "Please Mom, we can ride home with Jaye's sister", I talked myself into this plan. "Why not? They were good kids. They never give me any trouble. It's an innocent ballgame. What's the harm?", I reasoned. I needed milk for the fridge anyway and so I thought I could make this a "two birds, one stone" kind of trip.

I was wearing my favorite pair of sweats. You know, the ones that are paper-thin and you absolutely love to lounge in after a long day of work? In light of my attire, I planned on sending Hunter into the store to get the milk, which was a total win for me. At the time, I had sold my Tahoe to buy Hunter a truck of his own since he was at the age where he had his permit. I wanted him to be familiar with driving his own vehicle. But. I'm a short gal and his truck had a lift kit on it. The steps were "uncool" so He had gotten rid of them. Needless to say, I wasn't wild about driving his truck, so that night I decided to drive my husband's 3500 HD Dually. It had better lights and I hated driving after dark, so why not make it easier on myself? I didn't really like either truck, but it was the least dreaded because it did have steps. We hopped in and off we went.

As we headed out of the drive, Hunter and his girlfriend, Jaye, were all "goo-goo-eyed" in the backseat, as young teens in love normally are. When I got to the end of our road, I turned my right blinker on and began to veer right.

From the backseat came a roar, "Mom, why are you going that way? It takes longer and we don't wanna' be late for the game!" I replied, "I need milk so I was going to let you run into the Dollar Store to get some." His response was, "Mom, we will be late to the games!" In an instant (being the people pleaser, I was), I whipped the truck around and headed towards the turnpike so I could jump on it, whiz on to the game, and then I would get the milk later myself. Who cares if I have my lounge sweats on anyway? That tiny decision to try to keep everyone happy would change the direction of my life forever.

The drive over to the game was pretty uneventful. I was pretty much like the cab driver and they were lost in their sweet conversations and in each other's eyes. I pulled up to the Expo Center and they opened the door and hopped out. Hunter shouted, "Bye, Mom. We will come straight home after the games." The door shut and I pulled away.

I turned out the drive and onto Hwy 270, where you can see the Oklahoma State Penitentiary when you are driving toward McAlester and off I went. It was pitch black that night. I was driving along the road a few miles away. I topped a little hill and in an instant I saw it! Bam! I hit it! Boom! My thoughts were, "What was that noise? What's that smell? I need this truck to stop! Am I going to hit someone head on? I need this truck to stop! Oh, My head hurts." I had just hit a huge black cow that was standing broadside in my lane of traffic. I saw flashing lights behind me. *"The steps of a good man are ordered by the Lord and He delights in his way."* Psalm 37:23

I guess I went on adrenalin, at this point. The highway patrol that happened to be following me had seen the accident and was standing at my door almost immediately after my vehicle came to a stop. He could not get the door opened so he talked to me through the window. His voice was calming but I needed my family. I grabbed my phone and started dialing the people I loved that I knew could get here fast. I dialed my husband and he didn't answer, which was very rare. I dialed my daughter and she was on her way. I dialed Jaye, my son's girlfriend, and she and Hunter got a ride from a friend down to the scene immediately. I was getting sleepy but my head was hurting so badly. They were talking to me outside the door. The smell that I couldn't get out of my nose was terrible. I later found out it was the smell of the airbags that went off. I waited for what seemed like an eternity but the ambulance arrived and my son and daughter arrived very shortly after. I remember Hunter climbing in the back seat of the truck and talking to me, trying to calm me and telling me I was going to be okay. He was making silly small talk out of nervousness and asking me questions. After some time of working to free me from the truck, securing my neck and back on a board, I was in an ambulance. Hunter was in the front seat nervously talking to the driver and me. They wheeled me into the ER and the nurses and doctors began cutting off my clothes. I strongly remember thinking, "Please don't cut my pants! These are my favorite sweats....and yeah, I admit that they even have a couple of holes in the seat. But I love them just the same."

My husband arrived at the hospital and beyond that, I don't really remember a lot for the rest of that night. They were giving me high doses of pain medication and fluids, Xrays, CT scans and blood tests. They put me through the ringer that night. They fixed everything that could be fixed or patched up and now time had to pass and the swelling had to go down. The bruising had to fade before a clear picture of all of my injuries could be seen. So, I was released and sent home for what would be a totally different life.

In the weeks and months to come, there would be too many doctor appointments to count, surgeries, procedures, medications, physical therapy and shrinks. You name it; I went through it. As the days went by, I felt worse and worse. Dizziness, severe headaches, continual ringing in my ears and nausea were constant. I was uncoordinated. There were tons of things going on neurologically that I didn't understand. I couldn't remember simple stuff. For example, I had gone to town by myself (one of the first times to drive alone) and I was going to go by my daughter's house. I couldn't remember where she lived. I distinctly remember pulling over and crying like a baby. I was a Type A personality, always in control of myself, but this time, I wasn't in control of anything. I would later find out that I had a concussion and then as the weeks and months passed and the symptoms continued to worsen, they upgraded it to Traumatic Brain Injury (TBI). My brain had hit the back of my skull, then slammed to hit the front of my skull, leaving it bruised and swollen and for lack of better words, needing time to recover from the trauma. The pain in my neck was severe and it felt like my head weighed 700 lbs. It felt like it was pushing down on my neck very hard. I would beg someone to just hold my head for me at times to take the pressure off. I had severe fatigue but I couldn't sleep because of the ringing in my ears and the pain all over my body. I couldn't keep a thought or concentrate and my frustration would grow until I would explode in tears. I would have moments where I couldn't control my temper. The sunlight or even the light from a TV would give me tremendous migraines that would last days at a time. Normally, I would have to go in to get a shot for relief. Finally, the MRI revealed the extent of my injuries. I had herniated discs at C4, C5, and C6, which were pushing the spinal cord so the fluid wasn't flowing, as it should. Then I had herniated disc at L5 and S1, which were pushing on my spinal cord and slowing the fluid flow. I would most definitely require at least two back surgeries. I was determined to be the "one in a million" that could beat this, without surgery. I didn't have health insurance or med pay on my auto policy. Who knew you needed that stuff anyway? As time went by, I began having lots of problems with my kidneys and tons of kidney stones. I would have surgery to remove stones from one side and in a matter of weeks, I would have to have them removed from the other side. This continues although not nearly as often as in the beginning. I had injured my pituitary gland, which controls how our bodies react to vitamins. Mine had gone haywire, so it was doing crazy things with calcium and vitamin D. I was making kidney stones left and right. Days turned into weeks, weeks into months and months into years of doctor's appointments, hospital stays, surgeries and procedures. Throughout this time, there were so many days and nights that I felt secluded from the outside world. My husband took an out of state job to stay on top of the mounting medical bills that I was racking up. God had His hand on our finances and we were blessed beyond our wildest dreams. *"Give and it shall be given to you: good measure, pressed down, shaken together and running over will be put into your bosom. For with the same measure that you use, it will be measured back to you."* Luke 6:38.

My husband's job, working away from home, helped us financially but it also meant that I ended up spending lots of time alone with nothing but my physical pain and my thoughts. I have struggled with depression throughout this experience, as well as, some other times in my life. Yet through all these years, I have been drawn much closer to the Lord. I had finally dealt with all the pain

I thought I could possibly stand. About two years after the accident, I went in to see a neurologist who recommended surgery as my only option to get some relief. I didn't want to hear that. As hardheaded as I was, I continued to seek out other specialists but they all told me the exact same thing. Finally, after months of deliberation, I gave in and decided to go ahead with the surgery that the first neurologist had told me I needed. I called and began the process of blood work and all of the pre-op stuff. Surgery was scheduled in a few weeks.

A few days passed and I received a call from the neurologist's office informing me that he was unable to do the surgery. (I found out later that my surgeon had committed suicide.) In a few months, the doctor's office called to schedule me with a new neurologist who was taking all of my doctor's patients. I made the appointment but was skeptical, in light of what had happened with the first doctor. When he walked in, my first thought was, "Oh, wow! This kid can't be over 18. He's just a baby. I don't know if I want to let him cut into me and work on my spine!" So with this information, I left the office with his card and told them that I would call to reschedule my surgery. I never did. I just could not get past the thought that maybe God didn't want me to get it done. Maybe, my first surgeon's death was a huge sign that I wouldn't make it through the surgery. Maybe, I would get hooked on pain pills. Maybe, the surgery would paralyze me. All the "what ifs" just overwhelmed my thoughts.

I would endure tremendous pain for the next few years. Day in and day out, the pain was a constant. The good days became the ones when the pain was tolerable. The bad days were almost unbearable. I was so afraid that I would get hooked on pain medication that I wouldn't take it unless I was vomiting in pain or on the verge of needing to go to the ER. I had heard so many stories of people with back injuries that had become addicted to narcotics and completely ruined their lives. I was determined that I wasn't going to become a statistic. My type A, always in control of myself, personality added to that determination.

Finally, after 4 years of pain and hard headedness, I found a new doctor that I extensively researched. He said that I was "way past ready" for the surgery and he thought he could give me some relief. I so badly wanted to have a different life. After all, God had blessed me with 2 beautiful grandbabies by this time and I wanted to hold them and play with them and be so much more to them than what I was able to be at the present time. So I went ahead with the surgery. I was petrified about having it done. Fear would grab hold of me every now and again and I would really have to pray and talk to myself to stay focused on the end result and not my fears. *"Fear not, for I am with you; be not dismayed, for I am your God. I will strengthen you. Yes, I will help you, I will uphold you with my righteous right hand."* Isaiah 41:10

It was a tremendously painful surgery and recovery, which required several weeks of continuous care. It probably took a full 9 months before I was really feeling like I was going to live. Throughout all of the time of recovery, I have been blessed in so many ways. I have been able to count on my awesome family. My parents have been there anytime I needed them to sit with me after surgeries or during hospital stays. My kids have been faithful to help me with anything I needed their help with. My husband has been my "knight in shining armor" in so many ways. Lastly, but most importantly of all, God has been right here holding my hand every step of the way. He has given me a peace throughout all of the chaos that is my health. He has sustained my strength even though there were times when I couldn't even lift my own head. His grace has been so much more than sufficient for me. *"And He said to me, "My grace is sufficient for you, for my strength is made perfect in weakness. Therefore most gladly I will rather boast in my infirmities, that the power of Christ may rest upon me."* II Corinthians 12:9

I have found a much greater sense of who I am in His eyes and I have learned how to love who I am (which is something I have never known before). There has been so much healing in my heart and mind in the midst of so much unhealthiness in my physical body. It's almost as if He had to get me all alone, totally by myself, to do such an amazing work. I have never been a confident person, never loved myself, and never saw myself as He sees me. I have held on to so many painful things from the past and taken each hurt so personally (as if every single bad thing that has ever happened in my life was totally 100%, my fault). Through this healing process, I have been given a much greater gift than physical healing. I have been given the gift of emotional healing. He has given me a new song and a smile on my face, even when I'm in pain.

I have had time to process hurts and to address situations that I was always too afraid to face. His Word says in Ephesians 3: 20-21, *"Now to Him who is able to do exceedingly abundantly above all that we ask or think, according to the power that works in us, to Him be glory in the church by Christ Jesus to all generations, forever and ever. Amen."* I am free from my self-doubt; I am free of my continual desire to please everyone all the time. He has shown me just how strong I am in Him. I am not free from pain in my body, but I am free from so much pain in my heart and my mind that I am able to deal with the physical pain with happiness and thankfulness. I would go through it all over again to be in the place I am in now. I have since found out that had I not been driving the 3500 HD dually, I probably wouldn't be sitting here writing my story today. Though my body is far from being as healthy as I have faith it will be someday, my mind and my heart are both in a place that far exceeds any place I've ever been and for that I am thankful. *"Then Jesus said to him, "Go your way; your faith has made you well." And immediately he received his sight and followed Jesus on the road."* Mark 10:52

I am still in therapy and working toward the next back surgery but I am going to praise Him in the storm. He has definitely given me some treasures along the way. He blessed me with 2 more beautiful grandbabies, which makes 4 total. Jaxen, Piper, Hazen and Juniper are pure joy and they have brought so much happiness into my life during a very rough time and for that and so many other wonderful blessing, I am eternally grateful.

Made in the USA
Columbia, SC
03 August 2023

21186016R00076